YOUR GRADUATES AND YOU:

Effective Strategies for Graduate Recruitment and Development

Other titles from IES:

Measuring Up: Benchmarking Graduate Retention
Tyers C, Perryman S, Barber L
IES Report 401, 2003. ISBN 1 85184 328 0

e-Recruitment: Is it Delivering?
Kerrin M, Kettley P
IES Report 402, 2003. ISBN 1 85184 329 9

eHR: An Introduction
Kettley P, Reilly P
IES Report 398, 2003. ISBN 1 85184 326 4

Kirkpatrick and Beyond: A review of models of training evaluation
Tamkin P, Yarnall J, Kerrin M
IES Report 392, 2002. ISBN 1 85184 321 3

Resourcing the Training and Development Function
Carter A, Hirsh W, Aston J
IES Report 390, 2002. ISBN 1 85184 319 1

Chore to Champions: the making of better people managers
Tamkin P, Hirsh W, Tyers C
IES Report 389, 2003. ISBN 1 85184 318 3

New Directions in Management Development
Hirsh W, Carter A
IES Report 387, 2002. ISBN 1 85184 316 7

Work-Life Balance: Beyond the Rhetoric
Kodz J, Harper H, Dench S
IES Report 384, 2002. ISBN 1 85184 313 2

A catalogue of these and over 100 other titles is available from IES, or on the IES Website, www.employment-studies.co.uk

the | **Institute**
for | **Employment**
| **Studies**

Your Graduates and You:

Effective Strategies for Graduate Recruitment and Development

H Connor
W Hirsh
L Barber

IES Research Networks

Report 400

Published by:

THE INSTITUTE FOR EMPLOYMENT STUDIES
Mantell Building
Falmer
Brighton BN1 9RF
UK

Tel.   + 44 (0) 1273 686751
Fax   + 44 (0) 1273 690430

http://www.employment-studies.co.uk

British Cataloguing-in-Publication Data

A catalogue record for this publication is available from the British Library

ISBN 1 85184 327 2

Printed and bound by Antony Rowe Ltd, Eastbourne

The Institute for Employment Studies

IES is an independent, international and apolitical centre of research and consultancy in human resource issues. It works closely with employers in the manufacturing, service and public sectors, government departments, agencies, and professional and employee bodies. For over 30 years the Institute has been a focus of knowledge and practical experience in employment and training policy, the operation of labour markets and human resource planning and development. IES is a not-for-profit organisation which has over 60 multidisciplinary staff and international associates. IES expertise is available to all organisations through research, consultancy, publications and the Internet.

IES aims to help bring about sustainable improvements in employment policy and human resource management. IES achieves this by increasing the understanding and improving the practice of key decision makers in policy bodies and employing organisations.

The IES Research Networks

This report is the product of a study supported by the IES Research Networks, through which Members finance, and often participate in, applied research on employment issues. Full information on Membership is available from IES on request, or at www.employment-studies.co.uk/networks/.

v

Acknowledgements

The authors would like to acknowledge the assistance provided by all the organisations and their staff who gave us valuable insights into their graduate recruitment and development policies and shared with us their experiences. Also thanked are other IES staff, in particular Emma Hart and Charlie Bass, who helped with the preparation of this report.

Contents

Executive Summary

An effective graduate strategy is increasingly important to many employing organisations — not just the large traditional graduate recruiters, but also the growing number of smaller organisations that nowadays recruit graduates for various types of work. This report presents research conducted by the Institute for Employment Studies (IES), supported by the members of its Research Networks. It offers insights into how employers are developing their graduate strategies in the light of current labour market and business trends. It updates IES research on the recruitment and early careers of graduates, conducted in the early 1990s.

The report is based on a review of recent published research findings and analysis on graduate employment, together with discussions we undertook with a sample of mainly large graduate recruiters in early 2003. The research builds on the model of the IES Graduate Value Chain, linking the supply of graduates to the attraction and selection process and on into training, retention and career development.

Various factors influence graduate strategies ...

A number of trends and developments can influence employers' graduate recruitment and development. Externally, the main issues are:

- the larger and more diverse graduate supply from higher education (HE), in particular from a wider spectrum of educational and personal backgrounds, and with varied experiences

- a more 'consumerist' attitude of many students towards HE participation, and changes in graduates' views and expectations about jobs and careers

- a continuing attraction to many graduates of the offer of traditional types of career development in large organisations

- improvements generally in graduate 'employability', but still some concerns from employers about the 'quality' of HE output

- underlying strong competition for graduates, despite market fluctuations, and continuing shortages in some disciplines

- the greater use of IT and the Internet in the recruitment process, with implications for graduate 'branding' in recruitment and selection.

Internally, factors affecting graduate demand and careers are:

- the considerable and continuing structural and organisational changes within organisations, in particular the trend of decentralisation of businesses and more globalisation, and also the increased use of technology

- a renewed interest in leadership and developing leadership skills in graduates

- changing career philosophies, in particular: less hierarchical career structures in large organisations, the demise of the 'career for life', and more self-managed careers

- changes in the way learning is viewed and encouraged within organisations, and in particular for graduates, how personal and management development is delivered

- changes in people-management policies in organisations, which have affected how graduate recruitment is organised and managed, and also subsequent career 'ownership' issues.

... Leading to diversity in purposes of graduate entry and approaches taken ...

Although the main purpose of graduate recruitment is still usually to bring in 'talent', especially management potential, a number of other purposes can also lie behind graduate resourcing decisions. This is a consequence of some of these recent labour market, business and HR trends and developments. These other purposes can include graduates' specific technical skills and knowledge; their ability to be trained up or developed into specific roles relatively quickly; or simply because they apply in greater numbers to a wide range of vacancies (sometimes along with non-graduates).

Because of the more varied and multiple purposes behind graduate recruitment, graduates enter organisations in more varied ways nowadays than in the past. To help employers clarify their aims and expectations, and understand more about the issues in choosing different entry approaches, a graduate strategy framework or model was developed from the research. This model has three main dimensions:

- The first dimension is the strategic intention for recruiting graduates, or the 'business case', *eg* are we recruiting for future managers, or more immediate business needs?

- The second is the kind of internal organisational arrangements in place, in particular, how much corporate involvement is needed in devolved organisations? Where are graduates 'owned'?

- The third is the need to provide planned, structured development — how much is needed, how is it delivered, and when? Can 'promises' made about job experiences, training and careers be delivered?

Using this model, five main types of entry approaches were identified:

- **high-potential corporate management schemes** — tending to be very selective, for small numbers of entrants, with a highly structured programme combining periods of work placement, on-the-job training and personal development. Such schemes are likely to be 2+ years in length initially, and have strong management input from the corporate centre.

- **elite functional or business unit streams within wider entry** — tending to be where graduates are recruited initially into a professional or business scheme (see below) which 'creams off' the most able entrants for fast track career advancement. These are less centrally managed, and often focused on one function or business area.

- **professional or functional schemes** (*eg* IT, marketing, retail management) — tending to be less academically selective, often recruiting from specific disciplines, or with specific attributes, of variable length (six months to two years), and combining work placements and training or development. They are managed mainly at a divisional or business unit level (they can also have an internal entry route for existing employees).

- **direct job entry** — tending often to be marketed to students as graduate entry but not a 'scheme' as such, graduates start in real jobs, managed by the line or shared with local HR, given less structured development, often individually tailored.

- *ad hoc* recruitment (or 'just in time') — tending to be where graduates enter advertised vacancies, often recruited along with non-graduates, given a variable amount of development, usually informal, and managed by the line.

But a blurring of approaches

Although each of these approaches has distinct features, their individual distinctiveness has blurred in recent years, with the possible exception of the high-potential corporate scheme. Small employers are more likely to practise direct job entry or *ad hoc* recruitment. It has become increasingly common for larger organisations to be running more than one type of graduate entry (*eg* high potential plus some functional schemes, and some *ad hoc* recruitment), and to be recruiting non-graduates alongside graduates for some roles. Despite the talk of the demise of formal graduate schemes, in particular the fast-track type, these are still valued by many organisations, and are also attractive to graduates.

An increasingly important issues for many employers is trying to ensure a good 'cultural fit' between the entry approach(es) used, the organisation, and the type of graduates they recruit.

Umbrella approach

Where multiple entry streams exist, they are often marketed to HE under one corporate 'umbrella', with the graduates recruited centrally (or the recruitment is co-ordinated centrally) and subsequently managed in more of a 'federal' way. This 'umbrella' approach can have multiple strands, either catering for different specialisms from the start, or branching out into various paths at a later date.

This approach gives organisations advantages of flexibility and also helps to promote a distinctive 'brand' to students and HE. But there can be drawbacks where tensions between the centre and the line are inherent in more devolved organisational structures. These can make it more difficult to achieve the flexibility sought, and increase the risk of not delivering on graduate expectations about the 'development offer'.

Graduate recruitment and development activities

The three main activities in a graduate strategy — planning demand, recruitment and selection, and managing entry, training and development — which line up with main stages of the IES Graduate Value Chain, are each explored further in the research. The main trends identified are:

● Processes for planning graduate demand continue to have weaknesses in many large organisations. They appear to have developed little since our earlier research in 1990. Given that medium- to longer-term management and leadership of the business is so often the main reason given for recruiting graduates (and is used to justify the significant resources spent on graduate recruitment), the lack of effective HR planning seems a gap.

● The main change in graduate recruitment and selection has been the increased use of the Internet and other new media. The main impact of this so far has been at the front end — in company promotion, advertising vacancies, application forms, and to some extent, pre-screening. The effective use of the Internet needs further research, in particular more objective evaluation of its role in the various stages in graduate selection, especially pre-screening.

Also, more targeting by recruiters of universities and courses now takes place, as graduate output has grown, but many employers are also aware of the inherent dangers in narrowing the field, especially the effect on diversity. The benefits of developing links with universities, and also pre-employment activities as recruitment and selection tools, are increasingly recognised. There has been little change in interviews and assessment centres (other than more organisations are using them, including many small firms).

● Achieving successful entry (induction) is increasingly seen as important, though organisations adopt a range of different approaches, and draw different boundaries between graduate induction and their main development programmes.

- In graduate development and training there has been a shift towards shorter, modular training, often throughout an initial development programme and also action learning, and the recognised need to improve management skills training. There is a growing use of mentors and coaches in graduate entry programmes, and more responsibility being given to graduates for their own learning. The quality of work placements in schemes is seen by graduates as an essential ingredient, as is career development. Graduates are being encouraged to take more control of their careers at an early stage, but there can be difficulties in getting the balance of responsibility right in this area between the individual and the organisation, between the line and HR, and between local and central control.

Key issues emerging

A number of issues of policy and practice emerge from the research. The main ones are:

- **aligning graduate strategy with the varied business needs for graduates**, and deciding on the best entry method for different types of graduates recruits, and jobs or roles. The rather weak planning processes underpinning decisions on graduate recruitment can make this more difficult.

- **relating needs and entry approaches to the increasingly diverse supply of graduates**. Various entry approaches are being used, but there are pressures on some employers to offer schemes rather than only direct job entry, to present a stronger brand to the graduate market.

- **the need to make best use of e-recruitment**, in particular through more effective self-selection and pre-screening, so that some employers do not end up with too many applicants, and others too few.

- **the development of an 'umbrella' approach**, which can offer varied careers to graduates in different business divisions or functions. At its best, this approach can provide advantages of centralisation with the flexibility of devolution. At its worst, it can lead to graduate entry schemes which look exciting, but fail to deliver on the ground (in terms of careers or development promises).

- **attracting and developing high-potential graduates.** A number of options are available to employers to suit their different needs and cultures. This also can include building in an appropriate international dimension to graduate careers.

- **avoiding overselling on the graduate development promise.** Competition from the market, the greater use of IT in the recruitment process, and the challenges in delivering career management in more complex and often volatile organisations, have increased the dangers of this. On the more positive side, stronger links are being facilitated between graduate development and management development through more modular training and encouragement of self-development in graduate entrants.

- **deciding on the right balance between the centre and the line** in large devolved organisations, so that the various elements of graduate recruitment and development can be effectively delivered. Such organisations may need to consider more of a federal approach to managing graduate entry and development in the future.

The future

The report ends by suggesting a number of issues on the horizon which are likely to shape future graduate strategies. These are:

- expected further changes in graduate supply, due to government HE policy, and also the changing interface between HE and employment

- continuing difficulties expected in recruiting science, engineering and technology graduates, due to little change in the numbers taking degrees in these subjects

- increasing international mobility demanded from graduates, and also a larger, international pool of potential recruits

- the expansion and development of IT in recruitment. This will require a better assessment than currently available on its effectiveness, and in particular its use in pre-screening.

- higher expectations from graduates about the 'development offer', and the use of more imaginative and varied forms of learning.

1. Introduction

This research, sponsored by IES Resourcing and Organisation Research Network members, explores employers' graduate strategies in a changing world.

Employers today want graduates for a variety of reasons, and different strategic intentions generally lie behind graduate entry programmes. These depend on how organisations see their needs for graduates as well as their structures and cultures, and also the supply of graduates and their aspirations. It can be a difficult process for organisations to get right, especially large ones recruiting for increasingly diverse business needs, or those currently experiencing major business or structural upheavals. It often needs to involve people in both HR and the line and also some forward planning. IES believes it is helpful to see the various elements of a graduate strategy as links in the IES Graduate Value Chain, as shown in Figure 1.1.

Various research studies look at individual elements in the chain, for example graduate recruitment, selection, development, retention, but few provide an overarching view of how they fit

Figure 1.1: The IES Graduate Value Chain

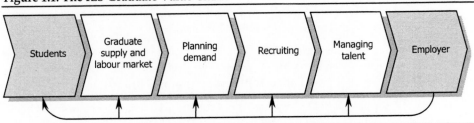

Source: IES, 2003

together in a coherent graduate strategy for an organisation. This was the focus of this study.

1.1 Research aim and method

The primary aim of this research was to explore how approaches to graduate recruitment and development are changing in the light of business, labour market and other changes. It sought to identify current issues for employers in developing effective graduate strategies. During the 1990s, IES undertook research on graduate entry and career development, and also on the early career paths of graduates (Connor, Strebler and Hirsh, 1991; Connor and Pollard, 1996), and more recently on graduate retention (Tyers, Perryman and Barber, 2003) and on management development (Hirsh and Carter, 2002). This research updated the earlier research and also built on the other, more recent IES work on graduates.

The IES Graduate Value Chain was used to develop a graduate strategy model, which enabled key issues to be discussed with employers. This is shown in Figure 1.2.

The project had three main phases:

- a Research Network forum in September 2002, attended by some 25 employers, where key issues were discussed and practice shared. As preparation for this, an email inquiry was conducted among Network members to provide some contrasting examples of graduate approaches and current issues.

- a review of recent literature to identify relevant research, especially employer-based case study evidence

- interviews in a sample of employing organisations across a range of sectors (public, financial retail, engineering, leisure) and of varying depth and focus. In most of them, they included managers responsible for graduate recruitment and development, line managers of new graduates and also, in a few places, some graduates themselves. They included:

  - Scottish and Newcastle plc: a large international drinks and retail group, where we focused on a new international graduate recruitment programme (trans-Europe)

  - ASDA plc: a national supermarket chain recruiting graduates to retail store management and also to other functions

Figure 1.2: Graduate strategy model

Graduate Strategy			
Understanding graduate supply and the labour market	**Planning demand for graduates**	**Graduate recruitment and selection**	**Graduate entry, training and development**
How is the supply of new graduates changing? What are the demand trends? Where are there labour market pressures? What are the most effective recruitment methods? What should we be benchmarking? Are there other graduates we can recruit, from elsewhere?	Why are we taking graduates? For what kinds of jobs? Where do graduates fit within our wider resourcing strategy? How many do we need? What skills do we want? So what kind of graduates will we target?	How do we find the graduates we want? What are we looking for? What is best selection method to use? What kind of offer to make?	What aspects of the recruitment 'offer' are most critical to deliver? What skill development do they need, and how will it be delivered? How will we manage them? And retain them? What careers options will we offer? How will career moves be managed?

Left axis label: **Higher education and graduates**
Right axis label: **Employers**

Source: IES, 2003

- Corus plc: an international steel production group, recruiting engineers and technologists to several, mainly UK, sites

- Sigmer Technologies Ltd: a small software systems company recruiting technical graduates on an occasional basis

- the Prison Service, which is developing a new scheme offering multiple entry routes to senior operational posts for both graduates and internal recruits

- a large and diverse hi-tech engineering group, where we focused on graduate recruitment into the electronics business

- a large financial services group, operating several graduate recruitment programmes

- the Civil Service Fast Stream (CSFS), operating a highly selective graduate entry programme for various government departments

- Inland Revenue: recruiting graduates for tax inspectors and management posts (in addition to taking CSFS graduates).

We also drew from a number of employer interviews undertaken in the recent IES study on graduate retention (see Tyers *et al.*, 2003) — in the NHS, manufacturing and defence industries.

1.2 The report

The report is structured as follows:

Chapter 2 provides some scene setting, by highlighting key developments in the graduate labour market, and also in employing organisations. These trends have a major impact on graduate recruitment and development.

Chapter 3 focuses on the various dimensions of employers graduate strategies — their distinguishing features and rationale for them being chosen by employers — and also the main changes in policy and practice over the last few years.

Chapter 4 identifies a number of issues of policy and practice emerging from the research

Chapter 5 then looks ahead by summarising recent trends, and identifies a number of issues for the future.

2. Scene Setting

There are many pressures on employers to have effective graduate strategies. Before discussing the various approaches taken, we highlight in this chapter a number of the key contextual trends and developments — both externally in the labour market, and internally within organisations — that can have a strong influence on graduate recruitment and development policies. These are drawn mainly from our own research studies at IES and other relevant research literature.

2.1 Trends in the graduate labour market

2.1.1 Larger and more diverse graduate supply

As has been shown in recent IES research (see the IES Annual Graduate Review: Perryman, 2003), higher education (HE) has grown substantially over the last decade or so, and now draws from a wider pool than ever before. Over one-third of young people (18/19 years) now go on to HE study, and HE students come from a broader set of backgrounds than previously, in terms of gender, age, ethnicity and prior education. However, there is still a social imbalance, as the majority of HE students come from higher social class backgrounds) see IES research for the DFEE, Connor and Dewson, 2001).

A graduate is a much more common commodity these days — over 270,000 gained first degrees at UK institutions last year (plus a further 150,000 postgraduate qualifications and just under 90,000 sub-degree qualifications). Furthermore, around a quarter of all economically-active people in England are now qualified to level 4 or above (*nb* level 4 includes all qualifications above 'A' levels or equivalent).

Linked to student diversity is the greater diversity in universities' offerings in terms of qualifications and subjects to study, and in students' experiences. The HE sector has become more differentiated, especially at an institutional and subject level, and is likely to become more so in the future if current government funding plans are implemented (see DfES White Paper, January 2003, on the future of higher education).

Other important trends are:

- more students now stay closer to home to study (partly because more are older)
- more are preferring to seek jobs in their local or regional labour market
- more are likely to have financial debt on graduation
- more are likely to have been working while studying, usually in fairly low-skilled jobs to supplement their income (over half of full-time degree students work during term time, some for well over 15 hours per week). Though working during term time can affect study, it means that more students have some kind of work experience when they apply for jobs on graduation.

From an employer perspective, these trends in graduate supply have mainly meant that there are a lot more graduates around than a decade ago, and so potentially more job applicants, though of noticeably variable quality. One employer we interviewed commented thus:

> '… there are "layers" of students coming out now, not all can compete for the best jobs, and some take a while to realise that they are not in the top layer and need to lower their sights.'

2.1.2 Developing 'employability' in HE

A few years ago, one of the main criticisms from employers of new graduates was their lack of preparedness for the world of work, and lack of generic skills (Dearing Review, 1997; Harvey *et al.*, 1997). To try to counter this, more emphasis has been put on developing students' employability while in HE, through various curriculum initiatives. These have met with some success to date, but it is uncertain how much graduate employability has actually improved as a result. This may be due in part to a continuing lack of clarity and consensus about what key attributes or 'core' or 'key' skills employers want to see in new graduates, and confusion on terminology (see IES research by Hillage and Pollard, 1998 on developing an employability framework). There have also been difficulties in actually making significant changes to the curriculum of academic courses (Hesketh, 2000). The recent SkillsPlus project (part of HEFCE's HE Innovations Programme) appears to offer some practical ideas about how to develop employability within the HE curriculum, in ways both relevant to employers and consistent with traditional values and expectations of academics. (Knight and Yorke, 2001). This work is likely to be developed further.

2.1.3 Diverse demand but underlying trends are still strong

Although it can be difficult to generalise because of the breadth and diversity in the graduate market, overall demand for graduates does not appear to have weakened significantly over the last few years. Underlying demand for graduates is still healthy, and competition generally strong, though there have been fluctuations in certain sectors from time to time (notably the downturn in IT last year, after several years of fast growth that meant its recruitment problems virtually disappeared). Despite the growth in supply, some recruiters, in particular those seeking scientific and technical graduates or very high-potential candidates, do continue to experience supply shortages.

The recruitment market in 2002 eased a little, but indications are that it has picked up again in 2003, as reported by the AGR who represent the larger UK employers (AGR, 2003). This easing last year was thought to be mainly a combination of supply-side improvements and the slight downturn in graduate vacancies, which was partly economy (including '9/11') related. It has also been suggested that improved university targeting by employers helped companies meet their target intakes (see CSU, 2002).

For those recruiters who are seeking a small number of high calibre candidates, the market is as competitive as ever, despite the expanding graduate output. This represents, though, only a small part of the total graduate market, which is very diverse, and employers' and graduates' experiences can vary. The vast majority of graduates are sought for, and enter, a wide range of jobs and training programmes. This includes many new graduate occupations, which may be relatively low-skilled occupations compared to the traditional areas of new-graduate employment, but are often seen as appropriate by graduates themselves (Purcell, Pitcher and Simm, 1999). Also, an increasing number of graduates go into small firms (it is estimated that at least a quarter now go into firms employing fewer than 50 people), and find them attractive places.

Recent IES research for HERDA-SW[1] (Perryman *et al.*, 2003), reported that the micro environment in smaller organisations often provided freedom for flexible, informal skill development, which contrasts with opportunities in larger organisations, where graduates may have to compete with others.

2.1.4 Recruiting in an electronic age

One traditional indicator of graduate demand has been the level of advertised vacancies, but this is now less meaningful because of the growth in use of the Internet in graduate advertising and recruitment (see the IES Annual Graduate Review: Perryman, 2003). There is also more year-round recruitment, where employers go out to the marketplace when they have a vacancy rather than planning a large recruitment campaign.

The increased popularity of e-recruitment for graduates has been the single main area of change to graduate recruitment methods in the last few years:

- It is now reported as the most useful graduate recruiting tool (AGR, 2002), a marked change from the situation only two or three years ago.

- Most graduate recruiters have dedicated websites and almost all use the Internet for advertising vacancies (AGR, 2002).

- A growing number of recruiters are moving to 100 per cent online application for graduates (*ie* replacing paper-based systems), including some pre-selection (online tests or telephone interview).

---

[1] Higher Education Regional Development Agency — South West

- A growing number of websites are gateways to information about recruiters and job vacancies, provided by individual university careers services, CSU Prospects and commercial agencies

- many university graduate careers services now routinely email final year students about vacancies and also employers likely to be of particular interest to them.

- More employers are using multimedia (*eg* CDs) to communicate information that previously was mainly found in their brochures (which are themselves less common).

An IES survey of final year students in South West HE Institutions, showed that 83 per cent of students studying full time and 35 per cent studying part time had used the Internet to improve their employability (Perryman *et al.*, 2003).

The greater use of IT in graduate recruitment and selection has many implications for resourcing strategies generally (see Kerrin and Kettley, 2003). In particular, in graduate recruitment it can:

- improve student access to information about possible employers and careers, and the quality of such information, especially on what jobs are really like. This can put more realism into the overall employment proposition and employer brand (as shown later in section 4.2, branding and targeting have become more important issues for recruiters).

- change the number of applications students make, or the way they initially present themselves to employers for selection

- change the way students make use of the careers advisory services in universities

- for employers, lead to more self-selection methods, which mean in some cases they receive many more applications, but in others too few, or not enough of the right kind.

2.1.5 International recruitment

More UK-based firms are now taking an international perspective on graduate recruitment, though actual numbers of non-UK graduates recruited into the UK is still comparatively small. Older international businesses are becoming more truly global, drawing their pools of professionals and managers from many countries. At the same time, many traditional UK businesses have extended their operations to other countries and are at the start of their journey in working across countries and cultures (Brewster and Harris, 1999). Graduates appear excited by the prospect of international careers (Wistreich, 2002), but managing international careers is notoriously challenging.

2.2 Graduates attitudes and aspirations

2.2.1 Generation X and Y

Changes in the views and expectations of young people about jobs and working, in particular their career ambitions and achieving work-life balance, have been documented in several studies (Winter and Jackson, 1999; Sturges and Guest, 1999). Thus, the attitudes of many of today's graduates — those born between the 60s and 80s, who belong to what is termed generations X and Y — to starting work, are likely to be different from earlier generations. There has been much speculation and debate about the transactional and self-seeking behaviour of 'Xers' and 'Yers' — their thirst for novelty and immediacy, and control, yet without responsibility; and their likely different aspirations, which means they operate a very different psychological contract to that of their parents, the baby-boomers. The boomers grew up at a time when the economy relied upon making rather than buying and an employment proposition that was grounded in the notion of loyalty and jobs for life. However, it is worth noting that a good number of Xers will have already penetrated the graduate labour market some time ago, and may themselves currently be influencing corporate decision-making or setting policy agendas.

Comparatively little research evidence exists on trends in new graduates' attitudes. It is apparent though, from research with current and prospective students, that students' demands and expectations of university are changing (Rolfe, 2001; Connor and Dewson, 2001; Callender, 2003). More of today's graduates have taken a consumerist approach towards their university education, and more are motivated to go to university for career reasons than in the past. On the whole, they are less interested in student lifestyle and less concerned with the intellectual content of their subject, and more interested in the vocational aspects and their grades or class of degree. Another finding is that they are less willing to undertake independent study and more demanding of teaching staff time (want spoon-feeding). However, as with other aspects of HE research, there is likely to be considerable diversity in students' views.

2.2.2 Students' views of employment outcomes

Most students start their university courses with high hopes for their future career, and, as mentioned above, take a more instrumental approach to HE participation. This is more evident among young students from non-traditional backgrounds (lower social class, or less academic backgrounds). However, relatively few aspiring undergraduates have a specific career in mind at this stage, except for those in traditional vocationally-orientated subjects such as medicine or engineering (see Connor *et al.*, 1999). The options can be daunting, and there is a greater tendency for students to delay decision-making about job applications until after their final exams or even later (Perryman *et al.*, 2003; GradFacts Survey, 2002).

It is important that employers have a recruitment strategy that takes these trends into account. Although many students postpone their job hunting until after finals, there is a need for employers to start building relationships with students in first or second years at university, to help recruitment (Park HR/GEE survey, 2002).

The recent IES research in the South West (Perryman *et al.*, 2003) revealed a mixed model of job searching behaviours of recent graduates. Some planned to delay job searching until after their results were known, or felt they were too busy with finals and coursework submissions. However, others had made numerous applications during their final year, both nationally and locally.

2.2.3 Career prospects still an attraction

Several research studies highlight the continuing importance of career prospects in attracting graduates to employing organisations or particular jobs, as well as other factors such as early responsibility, the reputation of an organisation, a good training programme and good salary. This is despite all the talk about graduates being more opportunistic today, and seeking more immediate self-fulfilment (see above, re Generation X).

- A survey of final year students from pre-92 universities showed that the most common goal in career search is 'balancing personal life and career', followed by 'working in increasingly challenging work', 'working internationally' and 'building a sound financial base' (Universum, 1999).

- A survey of 2000 graduates, one year after finishing their degrees, showed that career prospects, ie 'getting on the career ladder', was by far the most important consideration for graduates taking their first job (CIPD, 2001).

But other research shows that traditional career aspirations have less importance to new graduates, and enjoyment in terms of liking the people they work with, being challenged and having enough money to afford the things they enjoy, were more important aspects (GradFacts, 2002).

The different survey findings are likely to reflect the different coverage of the surveys and the diversity of the HE output (see section 2.1) — the Grad Facts survey, for instance, covers a much wider spectrum of graduates in terms of institutions, abilities and backgrounds than the CIPD or Universum surveys. This suggests that traditional career aspirations may have less importance for the less-traditional student at this stage (though more important in general to them earlier in motivating them to go onto HE). However, we are constrained in drawing firmer conclusions by the lack of research evidence, in particular, graduates' views about careers. What does seem evident though is, despite the talk about 'new' careers for graduates (see section 2.4), traditional, structured-type career development programmes do still have appeal to many graduates (see also King, 2003).

2.2.4 Career plans change

Once in work, research has shown how the career plans of graduates can change. Many graduates start with a lack of confidence about the decision they have taken as to whether it is a good choice. The recent research by IES in SW England in 2002 highlighted above in section 2.2.2 shows the lack of preparedness of many recent graduates for the realities of the job they had decided to take. A Hobsons Europe-wide survey (Wistreich, 2002) showed that British graduates were more polarised in their career plans than those from other countries. The UK was similar to the whole sample in how many students had a definite idea of their career plan (21 per cent), but had almost the highest proportion (11 per cent) with no idea at all of the career they wished to go into.

Early career paths of graduates are diverse and can be quite complex for some, not just for those who choose to delay entering jobs. Many graduates experience a mixture of temporary jobs, further study and career jobs in the first few years after graduation. While often not in jobs which relate directly to their degree study or level of education initially, most seem to work their way after three or four years into recognisable graduate-level jobs (Elias *et al.*, 1999; Connor and Pollard, 1996). This highlights the importance of including 'first bounce' in graduate recruitment strategies, and also of not assuming that graduates' initial views about jobs and careers will remain unchanged over the coming years, as they get their first substantial taste of being in work.

Interestingly, studies tracking Generation X graduates as they move into their late twenties and thirties show them 'turning into their parents', as the demands of the workplace and domestic life lead to more conventional career choices and attitudes to work-life balance (Sturges and Guest, 1999). The demand to achieve a healthy work-life balance is currently high, and talented graduates are seeking this balance early in their careers. Regardless of whether we describe them as belonging to either generation X or Y, modern graduates (of both genders) are keen to seek out and maximise an employment proposition that offers such flexibility. Achieving a good balance between home and work can become more difficult to achieve as they progress into the organisation and long hours cultures and expectations present need to be overcome.

2.3 Business and organisational change

2.3.1 Business changes

A number of factors have led to considerable and continuing organisational change in many organisations, which have had an impact on the employment of graduates and planning their demand. These changes include the increased use of technology, competitive pressures and profitability, the development of global markets, and greater emphasis on service delivery.

Organisations during the 1990s de-layered, downsized, decentralised and became more internationally orientated. A flurry of major mergers and acquisitions were particularly prevalent in some sectors (*eg* pharmaceuticals, financial services). Some of the strongest brands in graduate recruitment disappeared or merged with their competitors. Organisations have adopted new working practices (for example more teamworking), outsourced more non-core functions, automated processes and systems, and become more customer-focused. Major new business systems (*eg* SAP) are providing new pressures to centralise and standardise business processes, sometimes globally.

In the UK public sector, the changes are just as great, with frequent major reorganisations in central and local government, health and education, becoming a way of life. The ambition to achieve step changes in efficiency and service delivery through the use of ICT can change huge areas of work very rapidly (*eg* tax collection, benefits payment). Public/private partnerships and the desire for 'joined up' government are breaking down the boundaries of organisations, and asking people to work in new ways.

2.3.2 Changing demands on graduate employees

These and other business developments have been highlighted in various reports in the 1990s that show today's graduates can no longer expect the same kind of jobs, work activities and career progression that earlier generations experienced.

- There is a growing and varied range of graduate opportunities, often in non-traditional areas, and jobs are evolving over time (see *eg* Harvey *et al.*, 1997).

- Employers have growing needs for graduates who are intelligent, flexible and adaptable employees.

- In organisations which are more devolved, information-technology driven and innovative, new-graduate recruits are expected to get up to speed quicker and fit rapidly into the workplace culture. They are also expected to work in teams well and have good interpersonal skills.

- There is a blurring of graduate and non-graduate jobs, and career paths have become more fluid (Arnold, 1997).

2.3.3 Importance of leadership skills

One response to organisational change has been a renewed interest in leadership and leaders — people who can make good things happen in difficult times. The interest in leadership is strongly linked with the idea that British managers are 'not good enough' (DfES and DTI, 2002).

The ability to manage people well has become the central preoccupation of many organisations. Important ideas have included the idea of moving from a 'transactional' to a 'transformational' management style (Bass, 1985), and the need to empower staff in order to motivate them (Argyris, 1998).

Some of the skills seen as being important in achieving a more transformational and motivational leadership style include:

- creating a sense of vision in a fast-changing environment
- motivating teams of people and leading through change
- being innovative in products and services and ways of working
- the ability to look ahead, to see the big picture, and deal with relationships (Clutterbuck and Megginson, 1999)
- teamworking, including the ability to work in teams which stretch across organisational boundaries
- a broad understanding of business, including global issues and competitor organisations
- being able to see what technology can do to improve performance
- dealing well with change themselves, as well as being change agents for others. This is linked with self reliance (Hiltrop, 1998), and the recently fashionable idea of 'emotional intelligence' (Goleman, 1996).
- Another way of looking at dealing with change is through continuous learning and therefore the meta-skill of 'learning to learn' (Winterton *et al.*, 2000), and attributes such as resilience.

Organisations are placing more emphasis on recruiting some people who will be able to develop to the highest levels of leadership. So we see a growing concern with talent management, often linked with both succession planning and high-potential graduate recruitment. However, there is also a growing recognition that many of the leadership skills apply not just to the top level leaders, but throughout the organisation, and certainly to all managers. They are certainly evident in the skill sets sought by graduate recruiters, and emphasised in graduate development programmes.

2.4 Career and management development

As already highlighted in section 2.2, there have also been some important changes in the way careers are described and managed in organisations, and the way managers are developed. Both these aspects of HR policy and practice colour the context within which graduate development takes place.

2.4.1 New career paths

It is difficult to maintain clear career paths in the kind of volatile structures many organisations have experienced in recent years. Downsizing and delayering has also led to reduced promotion prospects in some organisations, although vertical career paths are still a key feature of large organisations. In relation to graduates, this raises difficult issues of both selling good promotion prospects, but not overselling the careers on offer.

Some authors emphasise the need to downplay the career offer to graduates, and the more blurred divide between graduate and non-graduate careers (Viney, Adamson and Doherty, 1996). On the other hand, those graduates who enter through schemes are still offered a clearly differentiated career, with extra development to support it. This is in parallel with increased emphasis on short-term performance and early contribution to real jobs (Jenner and Taylor, 2000).

Although the promotion/expectation debate gets people very exercised, a more important issues is how flexible the promised 'new' careers really are for graduates. Talk of lateral moves is not always matched by support in the workplace for people who wish to make a sideways move into another function or business unit. So graduates joining organisations and hoping for quite flexible careers may be surprised at how conservative line managers still are in making appointments.

2.4.2 The self-managed career

During the 1990s, the idea of self-managed careers became very prevalent, grounded in the experience of redundancy in both the UK and the US. Those who take charge of their own careers, it is argued, will be more able to cope in periods of sudden change and possible job loss. The term 'career resilience' was coined for the skills and attitudes required (Waterman *et al.*, 1994), and the later emphasis in the UK on employability (see section 2.1.2) was born out of many of the same ideas.

Within employing organisations, the paradigm shifted, sometimes quite abruptly, from having your career managed to managing it yourself. However, as organisations did not feel entirely comfortable with this model for senior managers and those with high potential, a segmented pattern has emerged: managed careers for the few, self-managed careers for the many. This raises an interesting issue for graduate recruits as to whether they form part of the small group who will have their careers actively managed, or enter a largely do-it-yourself career world. As will be seen in the next chapter, this issue acts as a major determinant of the different types of graduate entry schemes chosen by employers in their strategies.

2.4.3 More tailored and personalised management development

Graduate development is, as we will see later, influenced to a considerable degree by how organisations are approaching employee development generally, and management development in particular. This is because most graduate schemes assume (explicitly or implicitly) that many of their graduate entrants will in time become managers. Even functional or professional schemes prepare people for functional leadership roles, as well as equipping them with professional or technical skills.

Ideas about learning have changed a good deal over the last ten years or so:

- There is wide recognition both in education and in workplace training that conveying knowledge through lectures or courses is not usually a powerful way of improving performance. The old idea of action learning, and the newer term experiential learning, place more emphasis on learning in the job, and through planned experiences (such as projects). This is especially so for the people skills seen as so central to leadership

- Learning may involve changing assumptions and attitudes as well as the acquisition of skills and knowledge (Argyris and Schon, 1974). The use of methods such as 360-degree feedback are often aimed at changing how people see themselves and their skills.

- Individuals have different learning needs, and will learn best in different ways (*eg* Honey and Mumford, 1982). So individuals need their own specific needs met, through more tailored forms of training. Mentoring and coaching have become popular ways of delivering much more personal development (Carter, 2001).

- Large organisations found in the 1990s that dismantling much of their management development caused loss of coherence and basic investment in management skills. There has been a re-strengthening or corporate architecture of management development, both expressed by competence frameworks and by core training modules at key career stages (Hirsh and Carter, 2002). However, such courses are likely to consist of short modules, augmented by project work and more personal support.

- Planned career experience remains the most important aspect of management learning for those seen as having high potential, for whom the intention is to offer an integrated combination of work experiences, formal training and personal support. Succession planning is seen as a process for identifying both career and learning needs for these groups.

Many of these ideas have migrated directly from management development into graduate development programmes. It is also clear that the development offer is seen by many graduates as one of the most important parts of their total employment package (Winter and Jackson, 1999). Problems can arise when the development expectations of recruits are not realised in their first few years with employers, in particular if the offer has been rather oversold.

2.5 Changes in responsibility for HR and managing people

The way graduates are managed at work is heavily influenced by a final set of background changes — who does what in relation to people management within organisations, and how changes here impact on graduate recruitment and development policies.

During the 1990s, as the HR function was often downsized, and also devolved, from a large centralised function into personnel or HR managers out in the business, many aspects of personnel policy were also devolved to business units to achieve greater flexibility, and meet varied business needs. Most of the management of people moved firmly from personnel specialists to line managers. This placed increased emphasis on the role of the line manager in managing performance, but also gave line managers the primary responsibility for recruitment and deployment decisions, and for supporting development.

As with career management, a central function has often remained dedicated to providing HR support for top managers (often seen as a corporate resource), and often also covering succession planning and senior reward packages. There is often also a corporate function responsible for the wider management workforce, for what we might call management development 'architecture' (ie frameworks and core provision), though most delivery will be more devolved. Again, this raises interesting issues for graduates as to whether they are corporate or local 'property' and therefore whether they are 'owned' locally or centrally from an HR point of view.

The HR picture is still shifting with the advent of the shared services model of HR, often linked to both a call centre approach to giving HR information and advice, and large integrated administration and data systems (eg SAP and Peoplesoft). Sometimes these functions are outsourced, and sometimes delivered by an internal shared service. The ability to re-centralise most personnel administration has obvious implications for graduate recruitment. Its application to development is trickier, as development is less about standardised processes and administration. However, organisations are experimenting with offering more development tools online (including e-learning and self-help career tools), and more development advice through call centres. As these services are typically available to the whole workforce, they will be part of the workplace environment for graduate entrants. Some employers are already considering offering tailored support to graduates from HR call centres.

2.6 Summary

This chapter has highlighted a number of background factors which have an influence on policies and practices in graduate recruitment and development, and the overall approach taken by organisations to graduates. They have included:

- changes in the graduate labour market — the larger and more diverse graduate supply; the underlying continuing strong graduate demand; some improvements in graduate employability but still some concerns; and the greater use of IT in recruitment

- changing attitudes of new graduates to their HE study, careers and employment; but the continuing attraction to many of the offer of traditional career prospects in large organisations

- various organisational and business changes, and the consequent changes to graduate requirements and demands on graduate employees; also how learning is viewed in organisations and developing potential business leaders

- changing career philosophies and management development — in particular less hierarchical career structures in large organisations, the demise of the 'career for life', and more career self-management expected

- changes in people management, including changes to the delivery of HR services in more devolved organisations, and how graduate recruitment and development fits into new HR policies and HR services models.

3. Approaches to Graduate Entry and Development

In the previous chapter, we identified a number of important trends and factors of influence on graduate recruitment and development, both externally in the labour market and internally, related to structural, business and wider HR changes within organisations. We turn here to focus on the different approaches to graduate entry and development, and how these have been affected by these various trends. We draw mainly from our case study interviews (see Chapter 1) and also other recent relevant employer-based research evidence.

Firstly, we outline the main approaches to recruiting and developing graduates taken by employers whom we interviewed, drawing also from the research literature. We identify a graduate strategy framework or model for describing different approaches, and we also discuss the main trends and developments in graduate entry and development over the last few years, and especially since 1990 when we undertook our earlier research at IES. In the second part of the chapter, we provide more detail on three elements in the IES Graduate Value Chain (as shown earlier in Figure 1.2): planning demand, recruitment and selection, and entry, development and training. The first element shown in that model — understanding graduate supply and labour market — has been discussed in the previous chapter, and there is little specifically more to say here.

It is worth pointing out that a number of the employers we interviewed were currently reviewing their graduate strategies and looking to make some changes. It is a dynamic area, and the examples we give here are therefore a snapshot view of current practice and issues in the early part of 2003.

3.1 Main approaches

Graduates enter organisations in various ways and for different reasons.

3.1.1 Why recruit graduates?

Traditionally, employers have recruited graduates as their principal source of professional or higher technical staff and/or future senior managers. Nowadays, although the overriding reason given by all employers we spoke to for recruiting graduates was to bring in talent, graduates are recruited for a variety of other reasons also, which may include (singly or in combination):

- for their specific technical skills and knowledge, *eg* to improve the organisation's research capability or for specific projects

- to enhance competitiveness (*eg* graduates can be converted relatively quickly into fee-earning consultants in a financial or IT environment)

- to help develop middle or senior managers — the talent or leadership of the future

- to help bring about a cultural change — *eg* bring in new ideas, improve the flexibility or adaptability of the workforce

- simply because graduates happen to be there — there are more available, and they apply to a wide range of vacancies.

3.1.2 A three-dimensional framework

From our interviews, we have identified three dimensions to a graduate strategy framework which help determine possible approaches to take to recruiting and developing graduates (see Figure 3.1):

- The first dimension comes from the business case for needing graduates, which we have called the **strategic intention** because it is usually time related or has some planning intention (*eg* recruiting graduates for long-term high potential, or more

Figure 3.1: Graduate strategy framework

Strategic intention	Degree of corporate co-ordination		
	Centralised	Federal (limited central)	Decentralised
Longer-term, senior management	High-potential corporate schemes, generally 2+ years (incl. international)	Elite functions or business streams	
Medium-term managers		Divisional, functional or regional schemes, can be run separately or under one corporate umbrella.	
Short- to medium-term professional			
Short-term, often for specific business needs		Direct job entry, but marketed as graduate recruitment/entry	Ad hoc recruitment (just-in-time)

Source: IES, 2003

medium-term, for middle management, or for more immediate business needs). This forms the vertical axis in Figure 3.1.

- The second dimension relates to the **organisational approaches** to graduate recruitment and development, and in particular, the degree of corporate co-ordination and control — where are graduates 'owned' in the organisation: centrally, divisionally, in business units, functions? Who gets involved and takes responsibility for their recruitment, development and careers: is it the corporate centre, the line, or a shared responsibility? This forms the second, horizontal axis of the framework.

- Along with these two main dimensions, there is a third — the extent to which graduates are offered **structured, planned development**. This often links closely with the first dimension, the strategic intention, since it is those who are recruited with longer-term potential who tend to get the most structured development, while those recruited for more immediate needs get the least. We have illustrated this third dimension in the central areas of the model in Figure 3.1.

3.1.3 Entry programmes or schemes

The various types of entry programmes we identified from our interviews and in the research literature, have been mapped on to this model (Figure 3.1). These were:

- **high-potential corporate management schemes** — tending to recruit from any subject, but very selective, targeted (high academic ability, leadership potential), small numbers, likely to be three years in length initially with a stated aim of achieving a post with high level of responsibility in so many years (often five to eight). Combines periods of work placement in different roles, on-the-job training and personal development, plus some management training. Usually a highly-managed scheme from the centre, also involving senior corporate staff.

- **elite functional or business unit streams within wider entry** — where graduates are recruited into a scheme (see below) in a function or business area which tends to cream off the most able entrants. This stream then acts as an implicit fast-track entry, often offering more rapid career advancement. Their initial recruitment may often be organised centrally, but with functional or business area involvement. Subsequent development and career progress is mainly in the hands of the business area management.

- **professional or functional schemes** (*eg* IT, marketing, engineering, retail management) — tending to recruit from either specific disciplines or to seek graduates with aptitude, interest or personal skills. Less academically selective, these can also be an internal development route for existing employees. Variable length schemes, from six months to two years, periods of work experience and training that could lead to qualifications for certain professional groups (*eg* CEng). Less pressurised than the high-potential corporate scheme. Often managed at a divisional, regional or business unit level. Individuals often move into middle management roles after a few years.

- **direct job entry** — tending often to be marketed to students or graduates as graduate recruitment but not a scheme as such, though usually they go into a recognised graduate entry type of position. Organisations seek specific knowledge or degrees to fill a particular need (*eg* engineering), or more general ability. Managed by the line, or shared with local HR. Relatively informal development, often given as part of general HR policies (*eg* induction, appraisals, personal development plan, *etc.*), but individuals can have their own development programmes.

- *ad hoc* recruitment (or 'just in time') — tending to be where graduates enter advertised vacancies, or are recruited via personal contacts with university staff. Can be recruited along with non-graduates. Covers a range of types of jobs. Graduates are given variable amounts of development, usually informal.

Managed by the line. More likely to be used by a small firm with few graduate employees, but also present in, for example, office recruitment in large organisations.

These different types of graduate entry reflect a number of factors discussed in the previous chapter, in particular:

- the growth and diversity of supply, which means more graduates are available, prepared to take a wider range of jobs and have different view on careers than many of their predecessors

- the increasing range of jobs open to graduates, some in organisations which previously have not taken on graduates

- importantly, the various changes within organisations, such as the changes to hierarchical career structures in large organisations, devolution of HR policies and services from the centre to business units, greater internationalisation of businesses, and increased flexibility required of employees.

We found examples of all of the various types of entry shown in Figure 3.1 in the organisations we visited, though we came across fewer examples of the elite function or business stream type and the *ad hoc*/just-in-time type by itself (generally, it exists in addition to graduate schemes). It is more likely to be the main entry method practised by small companies, which we did not cover as much here, but one example was as follows:

> A small, highly specialist software company, takes graduates as and when needed for programming work. They are IT graduates recruited from the university nearby. They are required to be highly competent on the technical side, with enthusiasm and good communication and client skills. Taking new graduates is a cheaper option, and the payback is relatively quick. The expectation is that they will largely take control of their own development, but the company provides a good climate for this to happen and encourages self-development and independence.

In a survey of graduate recruiters employers by Purcell *et al.* (1999), all of the small firms in the sample practised 'just-in-time' graduate recruitment, but only one-third had a graduate trainee programme, while two-thirds of the large organisations said that they had a graduate trainee programme. Furthermore, it was found that *ad hoc* recruitment was being practised increasingly alongside (or instead of) recruitment to a management training scheme.

3.1.4 Corporate umbrella for schemes

We found it relatively common for large organisations to be running more than one type of graduate entry (*eg* high flyer plus some functional schemes, and some *ad hoc* recruitment). Each had different objectives in terms of skills or attributes being sought, initial types of work or experiences given to graduates, and how far and how quickly graduates are expected to progress in the organisation (and also the extent to which this is articulated to graduates up front).

This trend was already evident in the earlier IES study in 1990, with organisations developing 'families' of schemes, and is also supported by other research (see Purcell *et al.*, 1999). The interesting development we found was the extent to which such schemes are marketed under one corporate 'umbrella' with graduates being managed subsequently in a federal way. It can be presented to universities and graduates as one overarching graduate scheme but with multiple strands which can either cater for different specialisms from the start, or can branch out into various paths at a later date. Some also cater for non-graduate entry. There appeared to be several advantages of taking this umbrella approach:

- it improves the promotion of the brand to students. For example, the supermarket group ASDA has a single website promoting the company's graduate schemes — the Talent Store — but recruits graduates into several areas, see below. In another of our case studies, a large financial group, which has recently been formed from a merger, runs ten separate graduate schemes, but all marketed under one banner.

- it can help to ensure that the key attributes, or success factors, that organisations have identified for their graduate recruits, are incorporated into selection and development programmes in different areas of work

- it can give more opportunity for graduate recruits to network with each other and help to avoid feelings of isolation in the first few months or year, which can be damaging to their performance, and can also reduce retention

- it can provide greater flexibility to organisations, which helps with business uncertainties

- it can help organisations that have recently merged or restructured to integrate the various entry schemes into the newly formed business.

> A large financial group has recently been formed from a merger of two large companies, which has resulted in a number of established graduate schemes running side by side in different businesses within the new group, in a very devolved way. The integration of these schemes has to wait until other aspects of HR integration have progressed. The group has very diverse needs for graduate recruits. There are currently ten different schemes, some managed by individual businesses within the group, others related to HO type functions, all presented to prospective graduates under the one banner.

However, some of the weaknesses of the umbrella approach are the tensions inherent in many devolved structures between the corporate centre and the line. This can make it more difficult to achieve the flexibility sought from this approach, and also more difficult to deliver graduates' expectations of equality of treatment and development or experiential opportunities across the various schemes or streams. This is discussed further in Chapter 4. It can also be problematic trying to meet diverse needs from too much of a 'one size fits all' set of competencies used in the selection process.

3.2 Which approach to choose?

The graduate strategy framework shown in Figure 3.1, can help employers decide which approach to consider when making choices. Most employers can see the potential benefit of having a high-potential corporate scheme, because of a recognised need to develop senior managers from this route, manage their early careers centrally, and give them fairly structured training. These remain distinctive entry programmes, though they have been declining in relative significance over the years (see below). At the other end of the spectrum, the tendency to recruit graduates in an *ad hoc* way to meet more immediate business needs, is mainly a function of the increased graduate availability in the labour market (as discussed in section 2.1). What can be relatively difficult for employers is deciding about the middle ground — *ie* the recruitment and development of fairly large numbers of potential middle managers or professionals or functional specialists with shorter likely career horizons — and also the boundary between this type of intake and the fast-track or high-potential scheme, which can be fuzzy. For this group (who can be substantial in number), there can be difficult decisions to make in choosing the best approach: *eg* how selective do we need to be in terms of identifying ability and potential? How structured and centrally managed should the scheme be? Who will be mainly responsible for managing the graduates' careers?

We found more blurring of distinctions made between different entry schemes than was noticeable in our research in the early 1990s. For example, one of our employer interviewees in the current study claimed not to have a graduate scheme at all, rather it had a 'direct job entry' approach, but in fact offered much the same development (and presented itself to universities in a similar way) to another organisation with a divisional entry scheme.

In this hi-tech engineering company, graduate recruitment and development is highly devolved. Most graduates are recruited by different divisions directly into jobs in a number of different work areas *eg* software, systems, manufacturing, procurement, and commercial. There is no graduate scheme as such, but there are some shared aspects of training across the divisions and business areas, and all graduates get a set number of training modules in the first two years (the exception is finance, where there is a central recruitment and graduate training scheme). It is up to the individual graduate to push for professional development (*ie* leading to chartered engineer status).

3.2.1 Decline but not disappearance of fast track

In some large organisations, we found new schemes had been introduced, in place of, or running alongside, traditional high-potential schemes (what some called fast-track 'career' schemes), which were usually on a smaller scale than in the past. It is important to note that despite all the changes that have taken place in organisational structure and demands of work, organisations still value, and put considerable resources into, this kind of traditional career-entry model as a way of developing their cadre of top corporate management, as in the two examples below. Also, as shown in the previous chapter, graduates attracted to large organisations retain interest in a conventional career of this kind. In one of our case studies, a new high-potential corporate scheme was being initiated to meet the needs of the business for top-level managers:

> The giant beer and retail organisation, Scottish and Newcastle plc, saw a need to develop a top international cadre of managers, capable of managing their relatively complex and more internationally-orientated business. Their preferred option was to start a new international graduate recruitment programme. This is additional to their various national- and business-based graduate entry and management programmes. It was not sufficient, they felt, to source this new management capability by going through their 'normal channels' (ie business-owned graduate management schemes, or recruiting managers with international experience). The new international scheme has a comparatively small and highly selective intake (around 60 over five years), across a number of European countries, and, through a structured development programme, aims to bring graduates on fairly rapidly to senior international management positions (within ten years).

In the Civil Service, despite all the changes that have taken place in its organisation and nature of work, the Fast Stream is a key recruitment source of future senior civil servants:

> A substantial amount of change has occurred in recent years to HR resourcing and to the nature of the work and skills required by senior staff in the Civil Service, but its Fast Stream (FS) is still seen as the most important route for new graduates of high calibre or high potential at the beginning of their careers. The main 'deal' is that the FS intake, through being given early responsibility and challenging work, and a programme of management training and development, can expect to get rapid promotion, reach grade 7 quickly, and make it to senior CS posts in around five to eight years.

3.2.2 Cultural fit

Another important trend is the greater emphasis now given to getting a good cultural fit between graduate recruits, an organisation's way of working, and its graduate entry approach. This can be expressed in terms of graduates' personal attributes or skills, and backgrounds, in addition to any technical skills they have and their intellectual abilities. It reflects some general trends in the need for employees to have greater adaptability and greater focus on customers and service delivery, but additionally a greater need for graduates (regardless of entry method) to add value relatively quickly to an organisation and its operations.

ASDA recruits graduates into retail management and a number of commercial areas. It is marketed on the Web as one scheme — The Talent Store — a three-year programme but with six different streams, each of which has slightly different content, style, management and expectations relating to career progression. A distinctive feature is that 40 per cent of their graduate intake is recruited from students or graduates employed within the business. The company sees graduates as an important source of new talent, which helps to keep it innovative and at the front edge of competition. It looks for a very good personality fit to the ASDA ethos and culture from its graduates, which includes having spark, resilience and flexibility. It expects graduates to take early responsibility, and to show initiative. Some, in particular those on the retail management scheme, are expected to move quickly (within five years) to positions of considerable management responsibility.

3.2.3 Non-graduate jobs

As mentioned already, there is a trend for more graduates to be recruited to jobs where a degree qualification is not (or has not in the past been) a necessary requirement. Though this is increasingly happening, because of the larger graduate output, often companies have little idea of its extent. This may be because centralised records of the qualifications of employees are not often kept, or because they don't have mechanisms for ensuring that they make the best use of the available graduate talent in the company through internal promotion. However, more companies are doing so, and are becoming more aware of the benefits of providing graduate development opportunities to their graduate employees (as in the example above at ASDA, which aims to recruit almost half of the entrants to the graduate programme from internal sources).

Graduates can also be recruited to traditionally non-graduate posts or careers, by the creation of new graduate openings in previously non-graduate entry internal development schemes. In the example below, the Prison Service has recently revised its graduate entry scheme by merging it with other management development programmes to form an Intensive Development Scheme (IDS). The aim is to widen the source of people it recruits, to be more aligned to the diversity agenda, and to offer multiple entry points to middle and senior management.

In the Prison Service's new ID scheme, graduates are sought to compliment those who progress through other routes, and also to ensure a constant flow of managers with proven intellectual ability. Competencies sought include leadership, care and concern for others, and communication skills. A new graduate is likely to be required to undertake a full range of experiences, as a Prison Officer, Senior Prison Officer, and trainee operational manager. The scheme is directed at filling middle management operational posts. In addition, the Prison Service has a small number of Fast Track graduates from the main Civil Service scheme, but they take up non-operational roles, and stay for limited periods only.

3.2.4 Regular monitoring and review

As mentioned in the introduction to this chapter, it was noticeable in the course of the research, that many organisations we approached were undertaking major reviews of their graduate strategies at the current time. In some, this was following major organisational change (such as in the financial company, due to a merger of two large businesses) or where business or new markets had developed (as in Scottish and Newcastle's new international graduate scheme). In others, there was concern to ensure that their traditional strategies were as effective as possible, in particular in delivering the quality required of the organisation's leadership (such as in the Civil Service). It was also driven by competition in the market and the need for leading graduate recruiting organisations to keep on their toes. These companies were keen to seek out good practice in graduate recruitment to benchmark against.

As a consequence, this research review on current practices in graduate strategies can only be a snapshot at this point in time. It also meant that while we could discuss with employers the nature of their practices, we were unable to get much of a graduate perspective as we had hoped for, as some of the newly developed schemes had yet to recruit graduates, or had only recently done so.

3.3 Planning demand

We now turn to look in more detail at the three main areas of activity in a graduate strategy — planning demand, recruitment and selection and entry, development and training — and recent trends and developments.

We start with the area given rather less attention in research on graduate recruitment, but which is a fundamental part of a graduate strategy — deciding what is a 'sufficient number' of the 'right kind' — in other words, the planning of graduate demand.

Deciding about the size of annual graduate intakes may have to be done up to 12-18 months before the graduates actually start. This needs to involve some forward planning and, because of the way new graduates are managed and owned by individual businesses or functions within many devolved organisations, it means it is increasingly focused at a local or individual business level rather than centrally.

3.3.1 What's going to be a sufficient number?

Traditional top-down centralised planning methods, *ie* those that use workforce planning systems to come up with an annual graduate intake number, have become less useful, for many of the reasons referred to in the previous chapter (*eg* more diverse needs for graduates, more economic uncertainty about future, changes in size and shape of organisations, changes to HR services). The alternative, a bottom-up or 'bidding' process from individual business units or line managers is now more common, but this usually involves some planning at a local level, which can have its problems too, especially in predicting business demand. It can also cause difficulties because of the way it can cut across corporate HR policies. For example, if no constraint is put on numbers from the centre, overall recruitment targets can go up and down according to local needs (which tend to be relatively short term in outlook) without any overall view being taken of realistic long-term corporate needs, or changes in the overall infrastructure of the company.

The uncertainty in planning graduate demand results in companies sometimes beginning their recruitment cycle with a fairly vague idea of the size of intake wanted, and views clarify later when likely job vacancies, and the number and quality of applicants they are likely to get to fill them, firm up. Some find this a preferred approach, as one company in our case study interviews indicated. In this case, it did not want to set annual intake numbers too far in advance and individual businesses then contacted students or graduates, who had earlier expressed interest in working for them, when vacancies became more certain. This saved students' time by not having to fill in long application forms for vacancies which might not exist (see below).

Corus, the steel production group, operates an online recruitment system. Graduates are requested to register their interest on the Corus website at any time of the year. This only takes about five minutes — giving a few brief details about themselves and their preferred location and function. They are then contacted with details about campus presentations *etc.* The individual businesses in the group decide around December of each year how many new graduates they plan to recruit in the following September. Registered students or graduates likely to be suitable for each available position, according to degree subject and function or location preferences, are then contacted by the individual businesses, and at that point invited to submit a full application.

Others typically aim to derive a good estimate by combining various indicators:

- outcomes of succession planning at a corporate level (*eg* how many will be needed to fill the top cadre of jobs in the organisation in five or ten years time?). This demand may be examined corporately, but more often at a divisional, regional or functional level.
- views from managers about likely vacancies and future needs in different areas
- experiences in previous years' recruitment round and numbers coming through the various stages (filter ratios)
- size of their recruitment budget.

The estimate is then adjusted slightly as the recruitment cycle progresses.

Yet others rely on deriving estimates of graduate demand at a business level from headcounts and available financial plans (*ie* focus more on short-term needs), or from their staffing budget, or based on numbers taken the previous year.

There seems to be no consensus about what constitutes a 'best' approach, and concern was expressed by some of our interviewees, and also at the forum we held, about perceived weaknesses in planning methods being applied to graduate recruitment.

Where recruitment is centralised or centrally co-ordinated, the process of setting demand is likely to be run by a central HR person, and usually involves him/her in some negotiations with local managers (*eg* the centre has to approve local plans). But where recruitment is done in a more devolved way, decisions on numbers are often devolved completely to a local level. We only found one example of an organisation undertaking detailed workforce planning or other statistical techniques in a central way to determine overall graduate demand. It was more common, especially in organisations with an 'umbrella' graduate strategy, that some kind of top-down planning process was in place, at a divisional or business unit level, to provide crude numbers. Often this was part of the division's succession planning process (as in the ASDA's store management graduate scheme, where new graduate recruits are owned and managed by divisions, *ie* covering large geographical areas). Target numbers were then pooled together at the centre. Alternatively, it could be done within business units, where each plans for its own needs and there is no longer-term corporate overview taken (*eg* the financial services group, with ten different graduate schemes).

On the whole, we found that graduate recruiters at the centre often had only a vague idea of how the numbers required had been derived, as decisions were usually taken at a more senior level.

Most organisations recognised the importance of aligning graduate strategy with business strategy, but found it difficult to accomplish. Balancing the long-term objectives — looking towards resourcing future top managers, and giving graduate recruits time to settle in, develop basic skills, and gain work experience in different roles — had to be reconciled with the shorter-term business needs, driven by efficiency concerns, where graduates were required to make an early contribution, and also graduates themselves wanted to take early responsibility. Also, new graduates are increasingly subject to the same business pressures of performance management. There were no good answers to what worked best.

3.3.2 What is meant by the 'right kind'?

Planning demand also involves what kind of graduates to recruit, as well as deciding about numbers. For most recruiters, this means putting together a person specification, based on a range of attributes or competencies to be sought, in a fairly structured way. This then usually feeds though into selection. It is unusual nowadays for recruiters to go into graduate recruitment without having drawn up such a person specification — a survey of AGR members found only a very small percentage used open or unstructured screening methods (Saratoga, 1998).

However, there can be uncertainty as to how specific to be at the planning stage about, say, degree discipline, technical and intellectual skills or personality traits, and there are obvious difficulties in defining 'potential'. Person specs vary in their level of detail on essential and desirable attributes (*eg* 2:1, numerate, has 'spark', energy, good communicator). The leading recruiters do this quite thoroughly though consultation with their business managers, and also use feedback from their graduate development programmes, and experiences of previous years' recruits, and trends in the recruitment market.

> When S&N designed their new International Management programme, they consulted widely to develop a 'graduate profile', bringing business managers from different European countries into the discussions at an early stage. This helped them to focus on what specific skills and knowledge (*eg* academic background, language skills, business skills) and key personal attributes they would find in effective individuals in the roles they had in mind for them (in the early years. The qualities being sought were, for example, 'identifies opportunities', 'delivers results', 'getting the best from teams', 'energy and enthusiasm'. This was then used to agree a more detailed set of positive and negative indicators in the selection process.

The need to have a good personality fit to the organisation as being part of the 'right kind' of graduates, was also highlighted by several organisations, alongside technical skills and intellectual ability (see the ASDA example above). A subset of this was the increasing focus on diversity, and the need for graduates to meet the organisation's objective for a wider diversity profile. For example, the Civil Service Fast Stream are seeking to recruit from a more diverse group of high-potential graduates, and one way of achieving this has been to review their person specification. Others emphasised the greater importance being given to soft skills in person specs, *eg* 'being bright and sparky', plus potential to develop into the kind of managers they wanted in the future (though the actual 'leadership' potential issue was often not well developed), good communication and client skills combined with specific technical skills. Several organisations developed their graduate profile from competency frameworks used more widely in the company.

3.4 Recruitment and selection

As has already been highlighted in Chapter 2, there is now a larger and broader supply of graduates, and the graduate market has become more segmented. This is a factor behind the development of different approaches to graduate entry. As shown in Figure 3.1 and in the discussion in section 3.1, organisations operating a corporate high-potential scheme have quite different policies on recruitment and selection of graduate intake than for other types of entry. They tend to be seeking a small number of high-calibre candidates, and generally do this through a targeted approach on a select number of universities. The increased supply of graduates has not actually made a great deal of difference to the experiences of most, as the size of the pool from which they seek to attract and recruit 'the best' has not changed, and competition is still as intense here as ever. But we found it had created challenges for some in dealing with the larger volume of applicants they received from the wider graduate pool, often really too many to handle effectively, as the quality could be very variable. Also, one of our interviewees perceived a widening of the gap between 'the best and the rest'. Others felt that, overall, quality was holding up, or even improving, showing how recruiters can have different perspectives on the scene.

3.4.1 Recruitment methods

For most of the rest, those seeking from the wider market, recent trends in the labour market and the growth of graduate supply have not meant any major differences in their choice of main graduate recruitment methods. This supports other research among graduate recruiters which shows that most use a range of different methods to attract applications, typically six or seven different approaches, *eg* advertising in graduate job directories, careers fairs, Internet sites, press advertising, campus presentations, *etc.* (IRS, 1998). However, as already highlighted in Chapter 2, the role of IT has increased substantially in the last year or two (*eg* websites, CD-ROMs), see AGR (2002); Perryman *et al.* (2003).

These new media can be very attractive to students. They also can have the advantage of reducing costs and time (to both employer and graduate), as well as providing a better 'shop-window' for companies to communicate a realistic employment offer and project the *right kind of image* to the *kind of applicants* that they want to attract (*ie* targeting, filtering out). We found examples of several innovative ways of conveying information better to students.

In a large financial services group, a CD-ROM had replaced the brochure format. It included a very professional film about four graduates joining the organisation, finding varied career options there, with an entertaining storyline and humour. This is very different from traditional approaches to graduate profiles written in brochures.

Recent graduate recruits to ASDA were being encouraged to post online diaries (uncensored) on a website to help give candidates a better insight into working there, based on real experiences.

However, e-recruitment can raise some challenges, such as issues of equity of access (Kerrin and Kettley, 2003) but we did not find this a particular concern to the graduate recruiters we interviewed for this study.

Additionally, other recruitment methods are still used more in certain areas of graduate employment: sponsorship of undergraduates, work placements, and recruitment agencies. Traditionally, these have been mainly used by IT and engineering recruiters, but some of the pre-recruitment activities (*eg* student placements, internships) are becoming more widespread, as in this example (and also discussed further in section 3.3.4):

> The Inland Revenue is piloting an internship scheme, with ten interns, selected at the end of their penultimate year (mainly 2nd year) for a eight-week placement during the summer. If satisfied with them, they will be made a first job offer. The expected advantages were that they would go back to universities as 'ambassadors', with good experiences, and talk about it, and also that they are likely to be more committed employees when they join after graduation.

However, there is no consensus about which combination of methods work best for which kind of graduate entry. Also, there is considerable variation between employers in the amount spent on graduate recruitment activities, especially marketing activities, and the correlation between cost and number of vacancies.

3.4.2 Outsourcing

Many large organisations outsource recruitment marketing and administration to specialised agencies, though few outsource all graduate recruitment. The greater use of IT may have accelerated a trend to contracting out to a third party, usually an external agency. They operate in various ways, covering different aspects: designing recruitment advertising, development of web-based tools, or taking over part of the administration and initial screening process (*eg* handling application forms, screening telephone interviews, organising and manning stand at a fair. They may work in close partnership with company recruiters (*eg* at careers fairs) and organise the assessment centre process.

Some of the large employers we spoke with had scaled down the size of their internal graduate team considerably (partly because the central HR function had reduced also), and so had no option but to make more use of external agencies to help with much of the recruitment process, in order to keep costs down. Some had outsourced for reasons of speed, expertise and flexibility of resource rather than cost. Others had chosen only to contract out some of the more routine admin tasks. They felt strongly that it needed to be retained as an internal function to ensure the quality of intake. One major public sector recruiter had recently taken a decision to bring back most of the graduate recruitment process in-house (except candidate handling) because too much inflexibility had been encountered (*ie* difficulties making small adjustments to the process during the recruitment cycle). Clearly, this seemed an area where there were some unresolved tensions, and where the quality of the supplier and relationships varied considerably.

3.4.3 Targeting and links

The sheer number of applications, however, has meant that more efficient targeting or screening methods have had to be deployed by employers for economic reasons. AGR research has shown that on average, the number of applications per vacancy to organisations in their membership (mainly the larger recruiters) is around 90.

Targeting recruitment campaigns on a limited number of institutions (15-20 max) has been a strategic issue for many large employers for some time now:

- it helps them cope with the larger number of universities of widely differing types and perceived standards
- cuts down on the number of applicants, and so helps to concentrate resources on those more likely to fit their specification
- helps foster closer business links with particular universities, say local or regional ones, or particular departments
- it can be part of a PR strategy (*eg* by always recruiting from Oxbridge).

Though targeting universities by academic quality is seen as a necessity for some recruiters (*eg* for high-potential schemes), it can work against policies seeking to improve the diversity of the workforce, in particular the representation of minority ethnic groups, who tend to be clustered in a relatively small number of institutions. It has, therefore, become quite common for major recruiters to include some universities in their target group which have a high number of ethnic minority students, or students specialising in vocational subjects of particular relevance. We found that questions of how much targeting, and which to target were becoming increasingly significant in graduate strategies, for several reasons.

- Firstly, there can be difficulties for employers of finding good measures of quality of output on which to base choices for their target list. This is partly because of the greater diversity both within and between HE institutions, but also because of their wide-ranging needs. On the whole, the large recruiters who practise targeting for their fast-track schemes tend to focus on university league tables on entry standards (*eg* 'A' level points), but this tends to ignore the huge variations in academic standards between courses in some universities, and also can risk missing out on very able graduates at less-academic universities. Some employers we spoke with in the interviews, and also at our forum, base their target choices partly on a favourable experience of employing a graduate from a particular university in a previous year. This also ignores the variety of output from individual universities.

- Secondly, there is concern that the more academic universities, which tend to be the focus of targeting by most large organisations, may actually have fewer graduates with the breadth of attributes employers are seeking in graduate recruits, than others. This was raised in other research on graduate employability (Harvey *et al*, 1997) and also chimes with some comments about causes of difficulties in finding the 'right kind' of graduates from some of our employers interviewed.

- A third issue centres on the increasing importance of diversity in HR resourcing policies, as mentioned above. Some graduate recruiters in our interviews (especially the public sector ones) had almost a mandate to include diversity in their graduate strategies, and be more open about it. Yet they were unlikely to be particularly effective in meeting diversity targets from their institutional targeting practices if these were too narrowly based, nor would it give out the public image that they wanted to have. For example, some were ensuring that they included some institutions with higher than average minority ethnic participation rates in their targeted list.

We also found several examples of organisations which chose not to target particular universities, as it would narrow down the field too much. Instead, they were prepared to handle large numbers (*eg* applications from 50+ universities) through screening techniques (*eg* telephone interviews).

There has been a growth in regional partnerships between business and higher education to encourage knowledge and skill transfer. Potentially, this could make it more effective for employers with regional locations to focus their recruitment activities more on their local HE institutions than spread themselves nationally, and so shift the focus of their target. We know of some examples of this (though not from our interviewees, but from other IES research). These include: an engineering company in the west of England and a software company in the Thames Valley, that has focused its graduate recruitment almost exclusively on local institutions and specific courses run there; and others who have developed tailor-made degrees at specific institutions (*eg* at Cranfield) and are developing their own new Foundation Degrees, in partnership with selected local colleges and universities.

3.4.4 Placements and work experience

Providing work placements for sandwich students, and sponsorship of engineers and technologists, has traditionally played an important role in recruitment to technical functions (as highlighted above in section 3.3.1). But we saw a trend for the whole area of pre-graduation employment to be used more in various forms as an effective recruitment tool, though employers may get involved for a host of other reasons (*eg* good PR, useful extra pair of hands).

Although there is mixed evidence from research about the effectiveness of this method compared to others, students generally find their experience of work experience or internships as 'positively influencing' their image of employers (according to a survey by Universum, 1998), and employers also have a generally positive experience (Harvey *et al.*, 1997). As one of our graduate interviewees said:

> '*I really enjoyed the sandwich placement (in a manufacturing company). I knew the people and the setup and I knew that there were opportunities for development. The graduate scheme involved a real job to do … I wouldn't be treated like the tea boy …. It was also an easy option as I got offered the place in January just before starting studying for my finals, I felt less pressurised about looking for jobs.*'

Most of our employer interviewees were positive about the benefits of such activities, and some were extending them. For example:

- ASDA identified 40 per cent of their graduate recruits though students on sandwich placements or working part-time in their supermarkets (and had target this year for 50 per cent)

- An engineering group participated in the Year in Industry (YINI) scheme, partly to raise their brand visibility (they took a couple of students each year after their 'A' levels and before entering university).

- A manufacturing company had started to offer sponsorship opportunities to employees who have completed modern apprenticeships, to go on a degree course. The advantages were that the company knew the individual well, and vice versa, and it was expected that he/she would have more realistic expectations about jobs and careers in the company than they found with new graduates.

- A public sector organisation was recruiting its first group of internships, as a pilot programme, during the summer vacation. It was hoped that these students would act as 'ambassadors' to other students in their final year of study.

We also found that a number of participants at a recent IES forum on graduate retention, endorsed the value of work placements as a retention tool, and a good number used them partly for this reason. They found that retention rates of graduates via this route were better than others because they have a realistic view of work generally, and specifically of their jobs with that organisation.

3.4.5 Selection methods

Selection processes usually comprise a number of components, and where relatively small numbers are being sought for high-potential management schemes or specific functions (*eg* popular vacancies such as marketing), usually have a number of stages:

- self-selection — via brochures or self-completion questionnaires
- pre-screening — by tests or exercises taken online, by telephone or face-to-face interview, or through scoring of application forms
- assessment centres and/or one-to-one interviews.

Self-selection

Effective self-selection is of enormous potential benefit, but until recently, organisations have not paid much attention to it. Simple signals are sent (*eg* don't apply unless you are likely to get a 2:1). More interesting are messages about the kinds of people likely to enjoy the workplace culture, for example: how important is teamwork? Will I enjoy spending time with customers? Are the hours likely to be long or erratic? Do you have to manage your own development? Will there be other trainees near at hand?

Brochures or CD-ROMs, websites and self-completion question-naires can be helpful in screening out those who may have the right background but would not enjoy the work or organisation. They can also screen in people who are drawn to the particular organisation, and can help encourage them more. One of our organisations spoke about the benefits of doing a lot of work at the 'front end' in order to get the right kind of graduates (those who have a good cultural fit with the organisation) interested in their business (which did not have a particularly attractive public image as a workplace).

Pre-screening

Some organisations have a long tradition of pre-screening via tests, though written examinations, such as those used traditionally by the Civil Service, have now been phased out. Tests and exercises to check for key skills (analytical ability, writing, numeracy) prior to interview, are used more nowadays. Given the importance of such skills, and the relative ease with which they can be tested, one wonders why such objective pre-screening is not more common. Internet-based pre-screening varies in content and intention, and is becoming more popular. Early feedback from employers suggests that online testing is helping to cut down on time needed for this stage, but not as much as they expected, as additional manual reviews were still needed for many and could be time consuming. This seems an area worthy of more attention and in-depth evaluation.

Most common of all is application form scoring — 'A' level scores, class of degree or other information relating to work experience, UK nationality/eligibility to work in UK, or responses to competence-based questions — as initial filtering devices (increasingly done online). For some, this can reduce the volume of applicants by a factor or five or ten or more in popular areas.

Some organisations pre-screen with initial interviews, sometimes held on campus, at graduate fairs or company presentations. These are reminiscent of the 'milk-round' interviewing popular in the 1970s and 80s, when graduate numbers were much smaller. They can be useful in getting the applicants interested in the first place, as it is often their first chance to meet someone from the organisation for a one-to-one discussion. Evaluations carried out by IES show such interviews, even when supposedly structured, however, do not correlate especially well with later assessment centre scores. Their function may be more to screen out candidates with very poor communication skills than to screen in the best applicants.

Assessment centres

Assessment centres remain one of the most established methods for selecting graduate recruits, often nowadays after a 'first-sift' telephone interview. They are increasingly used by the smaller as well as the larger firms, and can often be outsourced to a recruitment agency. The term is used to refer to a range of activities when candidates are brought together for a period of time, usually comprising psychometric and leadership tests, group problem-solving exercises and personal interviews. However, although a preferred method, many employers have concerns about the validity of their assessment centres, and are looking to find ways of ensuring higher success rates — in particular in getting the right list of necessary personal attributes and behaviours being sought, in the light of the changing demands of the workplace, and finding the best ways to select for them (*eg* through more role playing).

Assessment centres can over-concentrate on analytical and communication skills that are easy to see. It can be harder to get an idea of personal motivation, the ability to form deeper relationships, leadership potential, and the ability to work with people of very different kinds. Some employers have begun to focus more on seeking these in selection and offering further technical training to those recruited, in the belief that some skills can be delivered via training, but many of these 'softer skills' cannot.

Competence-based approaches

There is a greater use of competence-based approaches to selecting graduates, which has advantages in its greater focus on the needs of the jobs to be filled, and is also less likely to be discriminatory against non-traditional students (see Purcell *et al.*, 1999). However, if these are based upon corporate frameworks or past performance of graduates who entered via other methods, or are not kept up to date, such competencies can be at risk of being biased or discriminatory against certain groups (*eg* minority ethnic groups).

It is important that the competencies looked for in graduates relate to those needed later in their career as well as in early jobs. For example, strategic thinking and people leadership are unlikely to develop until graduates are some way into a managerial career, but signs of aptitude and interest can be looked for earlier, on entry. It is also important to look for specific skills and knowledge relevant to the jobs on offer but which may not be contained in generic competence-based lists. It was interesting that one of our case studies (the small software firm) used a very searching technical interview as well as looking for entrants with positive attitudes, communication skills, and interest.

A number of recruiters are moving away from relying too much on competence-based lists, to putting more emphasis on behaviours, so as not to underplay issues of cultural and values 'fit', which are increasingly important in graduate entry (see above section 3.2).

3.5 Graduate training and development

3.5.1 The development offer or 'deal'

Where organisations offer a graduate programme or scheme this typically expresses a few key elements of the employment and development 'deal.' The elements of this deal may include:

- the length of time for which the formal support offered through the programme will last
- the type of training and personal support that the graduate entrants can expect during this time
- the range of job experiences likely to be on offer, and sometimes some explanation of how these will be facilitated
- some idea of the career path or trajectory on offer. This can be in terms of where the entrants might be at the end of the programme, or where they can hope to get to over a longer timeframe.

As explored earlier, in section 3.2, there are different types of entry with different typical parameters relating to training and development, spanning:

High-potential corporate management schemes, which usually promise at least three years of structured development initially and may then link into further 'high-potential' development beyond that, if the individual fulfils their potential. Apart from the intensity of support on such programmes, their defining feature tends to be the wide range of work experiences offered, often in several functions or business divisions

Professional or functional entry programmes usually offering several work placements, but these may be in a single function or part of the business. The length of initial programmes can be influenced by the structure of professional accreditation, as is the nature of development support

Direct job entry, usually offering some structured early training and development, but more informally or individually organised. They shade into wider forms of ***ad hoc* recruitment**, not necessarily branded as graduate recruitment at all, and usually offering very limited planned development beyond training for the job.

3.5.2 Induction

Achieving successful entry of graduate recruits into the organisation is extremely important. Psychologists have long emphasised the importance of induction as a socialisation process, as well as one which imparts specific knowledge (Arnold, 1997). However, organisations draw different lines between where initial induction stops and the main training programme starts. Examples of induction include:

- A three-year structured programme in retail has recently introduced an initial one-week orientation week in head office to provide an overview of the business, before going out into an initial placement in a store. This helps reinforce the brand/culture and also helps to encourage social networking across the graduate intake.

- An engineering company has a very short induction (half a day), but graduates also have a nine day outward-bound experience to assist their social integration.

- A high-potential international management programme has an initial 3 to 4 week orientation to the business at the head office, before entrants move to their first placement in different countries.

3.5.3 Training and skill development

The type of training offered to graduate recruits tends to follow general trends in employee development, and management development in particular.

Modular management or generic skill training

Long training courses have given way to shorter, modular training courses, often spread throughout the duration of the graduate programme. For example, one two-year scheme includes six, two-day workshops on management skills. Another company includes four, three-day sessions in the first two years. Interestingly, this second organisation does not really claim to be offering a graduate 'programme' as such. However, it offers much the same amount and type of non-technical training as the organisation which packages it as a graduate scheme.

Such training modules often apply to all graduates, even when there are multiple functional or professional schemes. The content of such shared formal training tends to focus on managerial or generic skills (self-management, business awareness *etc.*). It may be based around a management competence framework used in the organisation as a whole, and effectively form the first of several levels of management training.

The inclusion of some management skills training within graduate programmes — and even for graduate direct job entrants — seems very common. It reflects the recent concern with leadership and interpersonal skills, and the re-strengthening of corporate management development architecture in recent years.

Training events serve a useful secondary function to get graduates together across the organisation and help them acquire a shared sense of identity and some friendships, and often form the basis for future networking contacts.

> For example, the retail organisation with a three-year scheme tries to encourage more networking in various ways — by bringing second- and third-year intakes together for joint events (lasting one day or less); and has set up a buddy system, so that first years will have a second- or third-year recruit as buddy. The latter, it is hoped, will help improve their self-management abilities, help them be more informed about what lies ahead, and more aware of the organisation's expectations.

While graduates are together at training events, they may also hear very senior managers give inputs on the business and its direction. This gives them some useful early exposure to business strategy, and also gives the senior managers a chance to see their new recruits (as one interviewee put it: '... *gets a graduate onto their radar'*).

Professional training

Nearly all schemes equip entrants with a firm professional or functional base. The only exception here are some high-potential schemes (*eg* CSFS) which provide greater breadth of experience from an early stage, aimed at developing more well-rounded individuals with broader outlooks, capable of both developing and implementing policy.

Obviously, those schemes leading to professional qualifications have a strong emphasis on technical training and experience. Their length, range of work experience, and formal training, all need to comply with the particular accreditation system. Some professional bodies, for example in engineering, also expect the trainee to have a mentor. This has further strengthened the use of mentors for graduates in some disciplines. For example:

In Corus, graduate performance is managed and assessed at regular intervals (every three months) with line manager and graduates agreeing an action plan, which is forwarded to the HR manager responsible for graduate development. Engineers have an additional performance stage, which involves progress being monitored towards IEE or other accreditation, via their mentor. Mentors and HR managers also meet at six-monthly intervals to monitor performance and progression towards chartered engineer status.

Coaching and mentoring

The widespread use of mentors and coaches for managers is echoed in their growing use in graduate entry programmes.

These take varied forms, for example:

- coaching from the line manager on each placement, to emphasise their role in skill development and business understanding
- mentoring from a senior manager, often more directed at career support and providing an overview of the business
- a younger mentor or 'buddy' to help someone get into their first role, understand business processes, and to find their feet culturally and socially (as in the graduate networking example above).

Mentoring is a direct way of showing graduates they are getting extra support. It may also guard against graduates leaving because they do not get on with their line manager, or find the job or placement unsatisfactory. If a mentor is there to spot trouble, they may be able to help find a solution.

Where graduates are very dispersed, for example in the Prison Service, mentoring on an area or regional basis can be useful. One of our organisations felt that mentors play a greater role towards the end of schemes, in the last six months, which can be a very uncertain and nervous time for graduate trainees, as they are seeking out or applying for substantive posts. They are also required for post-scheme support, to help deal with retention problems or under-performance five years or so in.

Action learning and projects

Action learning lies at the heart of graduate programmes — mainly in the form of full-time job experiences of different kinds. However, graduate trainees may also do other projects, as part of their management training or professional training.

Management education

It was interesting that the graduate entry schemes we examined in the case study interviews did not offer an opportunity to take an MBA as part of the graduate programme itself. Several of the case study organisations do support some employees in MBA study, but usually in mid-career. One company did mention that some graduates requested MBA study almost as soon as they arrived, and this ambition needed some managing.

Some organisations do offer an intensive Business School programme in the first couple of years of graduate development (*eg* the Kingfisher Management Development Scheme). The NHS Management scheme, for example, contracts with a university to deliver an education component (*eg* Diploma in Healthcare management).

There seems to be some evidence that employers have concerns about supporting MBA study for sizeable numbers of graduate entrants, on grounds of cost, unrealistic career expectations, and the tendency to leave the organisation at the end of the course (CEML, 2002).

Establishing a positive attitude to learning

There is a danger in graduate programmes of 'spoon-feeding' the entrants too much with training automatically provided. This is not in tune with contemporary emphases on tailored and self-managed learning, and so might not prepare graduates well for the wider learning culture of the organisation.

Some organisations are therefore giving graduates entrants more responsibility for their own learning. For example, one major financial services company holds events for graduates which they have to design themselves. They suggest topics and request particular speakers, and then the Training and Development function helps put the event together. If the graduates do not take the initiative and make suggestions, the event simply will not happen.

The example below reflected a genuine desire to create a climate for becoming a 'learning organisation'.

The MD of Sigmer Technologies, a small software company, is conscious of the need to set the right kind of learning atmosphere for new graduate recruits. This is done through:

- having plenty of reference books around the office, and a policy of encouraging everyone to purchase books or manuals they need

- giving each new recruit a mentor, who also supervises their early work, and is responsible for helping them to become competent on the job

- setting a climate of asking for help, and sharing good ideas. The MD often asks people about technical problems he is working on, to show that everyone can use good ideas from other people, especially if they have encountered the same problem before.

3.5.4 Work placements and career development

Types of placements during graduate programmes

The main difference between graduate programmes or schemes and direct job entry, lies in the provision of a range of early work experiences during the scheme. As we have seen above, training provision is less of a differentiator, and may well be the same for all graduate entrants, whether on a scheme or not. The range and duration of placements varies considerably.

- ASDA uses a 16-week placement in a carefully selected store — one of its 'Stores for Learning', as part of its graduate programme. Other placements over the three-year scheme are then related to the particular function which the graduate has entered.

- An engineering company uses a series of short placements over three months, before the graduate settles in their first real job. In this case, the placements serve as an extended induction to the business.

- The S&N international programme has an early work placement overseas, and offers between two and four placements over the two years of the programme.

- The NHS leadership scheme offers two placements within the NHS, each of nine months, with an elective placement sandwiched in between, which can be external, and even abroad.

The type of placements tend to follow the career assumptions behind the scheme. For example, functional scheme entrants will usually have most of their experience within that function, although they might be deployed across business streams. Entrants to specific business divisions will likewise mainly stay put, although they may see different aspects of the work of the division, and have one or more placements in head office. High-potential scheme entrants are likely to have much wider access to divisions, functions and locations (and even externally, as in the NHS leadership scheme). In essence, the scheme gives them a preview of the different career areas into which they could find their way at the end of the scheme.

The quality of work placements is absolutely central to whether the graduates themselves think the scheme lives up to its promises, but in practice often varies (as we heard from some graduate trainees in this study and other research). The literature on graduate development emphasises a range of features needed by good placements:

- challenging and interesting work, with the right levels of responsibility
- good supervision, including a line manager who is supportive and can tailor their support to the individual
- enough variety, both within each placement and over the lifetime of the scheme
- the chance to network with other people, especially those who are at a fairly early career stage
- some visibility to senior managers.

In one national organisation, we found quite a rigorous accreditation system in place, managed at a regional level to ensure standards of quality are met. However, on the whole, monitoring took place in relatively informal ways.

Career development processes

As with training, there is a balance to be struck between the organisation managing moves between placements or jobs, and the graduate entrant starting to take some ownership over their career direction. There is also a critical issue of whether the responsibility for career development is central or local, both during and at the end of the scheme.

High-potential programmes are usually managed quite centrally, to make it easier to give access to a wide range of placements, including in head office functions. Such central management also sends a strong early message to the business that these people are a corporate resource. At the end of the programme, local career management processes can take over, and this can make it more difficult to move between functions or divisions. Some high-potential schemes assume that by the end of scheme, the graduate will already feature in the corporate succession plans. This reaffirms their status as a corporate resource, and may lead to wider career exposure.

In functional or professional schemes, the graduate is often managed by a part of the organisation, and tends to get their job moves in that division. For example, the engineering company in this study assigned its engineering graduate trainees to particular divisions, where they were then likely to stay. Some functions offer placements and careers across the organisation, but within the function. Finance schemes often seem to be more centrally co-ordinated in this way, even in organisations which mostly run quite devolved schemes in other functions. The job moves of some trainees are managed on a geographical basis by an area or region within the organisation (*eg* in the ASDA store management scheme).

Direct-entry schemes do not offer the same degree of planned career mobility, and the graduate will have to use the same processes as everyone else to obtain career moves.

A number of the entry programmes we examined involved graduate trainees actively choosing their placements and job moves. Again, this is important in getting them used to the need to plan their own careers once the scheme has ended. S&N is planning to hold a career development event towards the end of its international programme, to help the trainees and the company look at individuals' future career directions.

HR and the line: shared responsibility

In both training and career development, graduate entrants are becoming more active players. The main responsibility for managing graduate trainees on the job lies with the line managers for whom they are working. Their mentors may also be a helpful sounding board.

However, finding suitable job placements, and the management of the process by which graduates get their first proper jobs at the end of the scheme is largely down to the HR, graduate scheme management, or training and development function. There is often someone responsible for graduate development at the corporate centre, quite often sitting close to the director of management development.

Where the graduate entry programme is an 'umbrella' for a number of functional or divisional schemes, responsibility can lie with a network of HR or training professionals out in the divisions or functions. They can operate together to manage placements and job moves, as well as shared training events, for graduates on their schemes. The amount of control the central HR person has, appeared to vary.

Graduate schemes offering a range of placements and career opportunities require active career management from the organisation's end, and this almost always lies with the HR or training function.

3.5.5 Retaining graduates

While some turnover is to be expected, and can be beneficial, unwanted graduate turnover can be costly. Recent IES research (Tyers *et al.*, 2003) has shown that the value of efforts to retain graduates remains high. However, most employers were found to be realistic about retention rates and, on the whole, graduate retention is not as major a concern today to most employers as it was several years ago. Furthermore, actual retention rates have changed little over the past five years. They are relatively high on average — only 14 per cent are 'lost' after three years, but this average can mask some very low retention rates (a quarter of graduate recruiters can lose up to 50 per cent of their intake in the first year). Smaller firms tend to do better than larger ones on average, but there is much variation between sectors. Salaries, offers of training for professional qualifications, formal monitoring systems, clarity about the 'offer' and expectations at recruitment, and successful pre-recruitment activities, can all help to improve retention.

3.6 Summary

This chapter has explored some of the current trends and concerns of employers in their graduate recruitment and development. It shows a graduate strategy model onto which the various approaches being taken by organisations to meet their varied, and increasingly diverse needs for graduates, can be mapped. This has highlighted the significance of three dimensions or drivers of a good strategy:

- being clear about the strategic intention for recruiting graduates
- having the appropriate internal organisational arrangements in place, in particular the degree to which there needs to be corporate involvement
- recognising the varying extent to which different graduate recruits need to have planned, structured development, and then being able to deliver on promises made about job experiences, training, and careers.

Five distinct types of graduate entry have been identified, each with different strategic intentions, organisational approaches, and amount of planned development: high-potential corporate management schemes, elite functional or business unit streams within wider entry, professional or functional schemes, direct job entry, and *ad hoc* recruitment.

There is a trend towards organisations having corporate umbrella schemes for recruiting and developing graduates. Also, the importance of getting a good cultural fit between graduate recruits, the entry scheme, and the organisation, is being given more attention.

The chapter has also identified various practices in the components of a graduate strategy:

- continuing weaknesses in the demand-planning process in large organisations

- the recognised benefits of developing links with universities and also pre-employment activities, as recruitment and selection tools

- the benefits of targeting universities and courses, and also its dangers

- the opportunities to use Internet recruitment to improve self-selection and pre-screening, and the need for more objective evaluation of these stages in selection

- the shift towards shorter modular training often throughout an initial development programme and action learning, and the recognised need to improve management skills training

- growing use of mentors and coaches in graduate entry programmes, and more responsibility being given to graduates for their own learning

- increased use of career development training as part of graduate programmes, and the encouragement of graduates to take more control of their careers.

Issues arising from these and other findings of the research are discussed further in the next chapter.

4. Issues of Policy and Practice

This chapter aims to draw out some of the main findings in the research and key issues raised for graduate recruitment and development, under a number of key cross-cutting themes that we have identified:

- how organisations deal with their diverse needs for graduates (section 4.1)

- how these needs relate to the increasingly diverse supply of graduates and 'brand' in the graduate market (section 4.2)

- the relationship between graduate approaches and attracting and developing 'high-potential' employees (section 4.3)

- the challenges of delivering on the promises made about training and careers (section 4.4)

- the extent to which graduate approaches should be centralised or devolved (section 4.5).

4.1 Diverse needs for graduates

As has been shown, most large organisations do not just need graduate entrants for one kind of job and one type of career path. The organisations in this study have varied needs according to:

1. job demands at different levels in the organisation. Some entrants may reach very senior levels in the organisation, while others may reach a career ceiling in less senior roles, or in specialist roles. The issue of career level is most often linked to the idea of 'potential', often expressed in terms of intellectual capability plus other attributes (*eg* communication and interpersonal skills, and high aspirations).

2. job demands in different functions or business areas. These may require different knowledge (*eg* specific degrees in science or engineering), and skills or interests (*eg* commercial acumen in sales, innovation in product development).

3. organisational culture and sub-cultures. Organisations are looking for a good fit between the style and orientation of the graduate and that of the organisation. Functions or business areas may have distinct sub-cultures (*eg* corporate versus retail banking).

Matching the approach to graduate entry with the varied business needs is not easy. For example, several of the case study organisations have defined a range of short-term needs (as in 2 above), but are also hoping that their graduate scheme is flexible enough to deliver sufficient numbers of higher potential graduates to create a pool of senior managers for the longer term.

Other organisations are pitching their graduate programme (or one clear stream of graduate entrants) at the high-potential career need (as in 1). In such cases, the term 'high potential' has to be unpacked, in the context of the organisation's culture, to clarify the skills and personal attributes which the high-potential scheme will select for. Often, the high-potential scheme exists alongside other programmes or direct job entry to bring in graduates aimed more at professional and junior management levels.

Some organisations do not feel that the high-potential type of entrants are suitable for the jobs they have on offer in the short or medium term, or the culture of their organisation. Even if such entrants could be attracted, their career expectations would be very difficult to meet. At least one of the case study organisations deliberately aimed for mid-level ability graduates with relevant vocational degrees as meeting the majority of their business needs. Some organisations are not really setting out to recruit 'the best' graduates, but ones with the right level of ability and ambition for the jobs most of them will fill in the short or medium term.

Setting appropriate numbers for intake

In organisations where the purpose of graduate recruitment is to recruit a pool of potential future managers, one might expect recruitment numbers to relate to a medium-term view of the numbers of managers needed. As shown in section 3.3, we did not find this link to be very strong. Indeed, this link seems weaker now than when IES did a comparable study over ten years ago (Connor *et al.*, 1991).

The lack of appropriate human resource planning behind the setting of graduate intake numbers is of significant concern given the importance given to graduate recruitment and development, a concern we share with several of the case study organisations. Even when the recruitment process is centrally co-ordinated, numbers are often based on quite crude 'bids' from business areas. This issue seems, at heart, political rather than technical. Such broad-brush human resource planning is not difficult. It is rather that those parts of the business which will take the graduate entrants into their first placements or jobs, do so within short-term business circumstances.

4.2 Branding and targeting in a diverse labour market

Making the organisation visible

Getting the right graduates to meet business needs has been much affected by two important shifts in the graduate market over the past few years:

- the much increased diversity of the graduates themselves, in terms of degree content, previous academic attainment, and prior work experience
- the use of the Internet as the primary means of attracting graduate applicants in many large organisations (see section 3.5).

These two factors working together, mean that organisations with well known names or strong brands in the graduate labour market can get thousands of applications via the Internet — but not necessarily from graduates of the type of quality they are targeting. Organisations which are not well known to undergraduates can find their Internet sites much less visited, and may have too small a pool of applicants unless they strengthen their brand in the graduate market.

Factors strengthening the employer brand include:

- being a large employer that sells direct to the public, in an attractive sector, *eg* large banks
- well-known names in technical sectors, *eg* pharmaceuticals, some major engineering companies
- a strong reputation as a good company to train with, *eg* some accounting or law partnerships, some multinationals.

Factors weakening the employer brand include:

- the name not being known to the public, even though the organisation may be very large
- well-known graduate recruiter that has been taken over by another organisation, and consequently has changed its name
- sector seen as low pay and/or involving long hours
- the organisation being in the news for cutting jobs or closing sites
- fragmented graduate entry, not using the corporate brand.

Organisations which need to raise their visibility in specific populations of graduates are still building links with selected universities or departments via campus visits, student sponsorship or work experience, or research links. Some national schemes, such as Year in Industry, are also useful to employers seeking graduates with specific technical skills. These more focused ways of building a brand in some sections of the graduate population may be more cost-effective for some employers than other forms of promotion.

Schemes as brand enhancers

The idea of a graduate entry scheme can be in itself a way of strengthening the brand in the graduate market. Some organisations which in reality offer very diverse — even fragmented — graduate opportunities, have found it advantageous to present these as a single umbrella entry scheme. Such a scheme also helps the parts of the business which are small or less well known, to attract the smaller numbers of graduates they need.

However, such umbrella schemes need to make clear what the different entry routes are offering and how different graduates may find an option to interest them. It is also important not to oversell the real content of the scheme, or to oversell the employment offer.

Other organisations offering much the same employment and training opportunities, present them as a range of direct job entry options. This may be a more honest reflection of what is really on offer, but does appear less attractive than a scheme.

So the answer to the question 'when is a scheme not a scheme?' is presumably 'when it's a brand'.

A brand with attitude

In this more diverse market, a positive brand does not necessarily mean offering only challenging jobs, rapid promotion and high pay — the classic 'blue chip' promise. Some employers have chosen to differentiate their graduate brand by offering different things, such as being a 'cool' place to work, fun, having different values, opportunities for travel, or state-of-the-art technology.

Sifting the diverse applicant pool

Organisations with a strong and attractive brand now find themselves besieged by applicants. One high-street name in our study has more than 50 applications for every graduate entry place, mostly via the Web. It dealt with over 12,000 applications last year, and anticipates the numbers this year being much higher for the same number of places. So how does it whittle these numbers down to a level at which likely candidates can be seen in an assessment centre?

Effective pre-screening is a vital ingredient of good graduate recruitment. Class of degree is still often used as a crude filter of quality, and also 'A' level points (*eg* 24+), but may screen out some of the graduates who would fit the business well. Online self assessment or tests are becoming more common. This is an area where further research is needed to evaluate the effectiveness of current practice.

Matching graduates to diverse needs

When the diverse pool of applicants is considered against diverse business needs, the problem of selection is more complex. Where an umbrella scheme is used to contain several programmes pitched at different business needs, organisations have not always clarified the differences in skills needed between business areas or functions.

Some recognise differences in skill needs, but still use the same assessment centre criteria to select all of their entrants. They do not necessarily feel comfortable with this compromise between their own analysis of skill needs and the practical constraints of the assessment process.

The process of allocating successful candidates to different work areas or career paths is also a challenge. Again the reality is often quite primitive — a combination of what graduates say they want early on application, plus popular areas taking the pick of the bunch.

Finding internal graduate trainees

Now that graduates are entering many jobs, not via schemes or organised recruitment programmes, organisations are taking more interest in finding graduate entry material within their current workforce. Such employees may have degrees, or may just be seen as of comparable quality with graduate entrants.

Some retailers have used to their advantage, the large numbers students who work for them, some of whom are encouraged to apply for permanent employment on graduation. Public sector employers favour parallel entry from within as an aspect of equal opportunities, and as a way of promoting more minority ethnic staff.

4.3 Attracting and developing high-potential graduates

The pros and cons of high-potential schemes

As discussed earlier, there are tensions between targeting graduate entry on the 'high-potential' needs of the organisation, and going for a wider intake, often through the umbrella type of approach.

In practice there are three options for picking up high-potential employees:

1. an explicit high-potential graduate entry scheme (*eg* the Civil Service Fast Stream). These are now often alongside other forms of graduate scheme and direct job entry.

2. a much broader graduate entry programme, containing at least some high-potential employees who can be identified later in career and fast tracked at that stage

3. an implicit high-potential entry group, focused on a particular business stream or function.

Explicit high-potential schemes have been found much more necessary in sectors or employers that do not naturally attract high numbers of able graduate applicants. Successive reviews of the Civil Service Fast Stream have found it important to the attraction and retention of some of the country's most able graduates.

Three disadvantages of high-potential entry schemes remain:

● the need to manage the career expectations of graduates who have been told they are 'the best' and promised rapid careers

● the tendency to 'crown prince syndrome', whereby high-potential entrants are bound to succeed because they are given so much more exposure

● the difficulty of selling 'ordinary' graduate entry alongside the high-potential scheme.

Employers that are able to recruit good quality graduates without a special high-potential scheme tend to favour option 2. This option has the added advantage of offering some flexibility together with a range of early career routes (as needed in manufacturing, for example). It also avoids the 'two tier' problem for 'ordinary' graduate recruits in an organisation that also has a fast-track scheme.

The third model is evident in the case study organisations. In one umbrella scheme, it is clear that many of the brightest graduates opt for the most glamorous part of the business, and that the company also thinks that is where high-potential people are most needed. In another company, an international entry scheme is, in effect, a high-potential entry. This makes the assumption that the senior managers of tomorrow need early international career experience.

Some organisations that have very strong brands, have found that they attract excess numbers of high-quality graduates on direct job entry alone. Some have therefore dropped graduate entry 'schemes' altogether, although they still offer high-quality skill development and professional training where appropriate.

Building-in the international dimension

Recent years have seen a growing emphasis on international experience in leadership development. Many large organisations assume that future leaders will need to have experience of working in more than one country, and to be proficient at cross-cultural working.

Organisations are managing this need in various ways:

- a very devolved approach to graduate recruitment in different countries, but hopefully bringing in some high-potential people in each main location, who can be given international experience later on (*eg* Corus)
- an explicitly international entry scheme, pitched clearly at a high-potential intake, and building in international placements from the start (*eg* Scottish and Newcastle)
- functional schemes with an explicitly international flavour (*eg* Thames Water engineering).

Links with corporate succession

Most large organisations have some corporate process for identifying high-potential managers in mid-career, often linked with a succession planning process. If there is also a high-potential intake through graduate recruitment, it is helpful to be transparent about how these processes relate to each other.

In some organisations, there is an expectation that high-potential graduate recruits will have planned development for several years, and beyond that be picked up by the succession system. In other organisations, there is a somewhat deliberate break between the two, to allow other high-potential staff to emerge. However, high-potential graduate trainees tend to be well known from their early career exposure, and often seem to retain this profile, albeit informally.

In either case, it is important that the attitudes and aptitudes looked for in high-potential trainees remain in step with changing demands on senior managers. The need for top civil servants to lead staff through change has appreciably modified the meaning of 'talent' away from a purely analytical skill set, and towards people management and an emphasis on service delivery.

4.4 Delivering on the career development promise

The danger of overselling

Graduate entry schemes have always carried the danger of overselling in order to attract good applicants. The move towards ICT in recruitment seems to make this even more of a hazard. The Internet makes it possible to put up materials, application forms and pre-screening processes which look extremely attractive and professional, and have the potential to mislead job seekers from the reality of the employment offer. Some organisations are producing CD-ROMs which are very attractive and sometimes innovative — for example, one of the organisations studied includes a short but high-quality film about a group of fictitious undergraduates and their journey through recruitment to entry.

There can be a considerable disconnect between a hi-tech recruitment process and the more mundane and challenging business of delivering high-quality jobs, training and career management on the ground. This disconnect can be especially great where the recruitment process is centrally managed, and the management of graduates, once employed, very devolved.

Career aspirations and career management

Graduates schemes offer enhanced training — which they usually then provide, and enhanced careers — which often fall short of the promise.

The career management challenges are getting ever more difficult as organisations become more complex, volatile and generally have weak career management processes (Hirsh and Carter, 2002).

Graduates on schemes generally expect:

1. a good range of early job placements, often within a business area or function

2. a good transition into a suitable 'proper job' at the end of the scheme

3. reasonably rapid career progression

4. the chance to move across divisions, locations or functions after the scheme (if not during it)

5. some clear mechanisms by which their careers will be managed, including strong input from themselves.

Devolved schemes can find it difficult to deliver on all of these. The biggest challenge is often the willingness of business units to allow graduates to move to other parts of the business, especially at the end of a scheme.

The processes for career management do not have to be complex, but graduates do expect the chance for reasonably regular discussions about their careers, and a significant input when job moves or placements are being planned. Having all these discussions with local line managers makes it unlikely that wider career opportunities will be explored. Some organisations are offering some kind of career workshop, perhaps coupled with some skill assessment, towards the end of a scheme, or finding that mentors can be valuable. This may help a more serious consideration of their possible future career directions, and then the chance for a more informed choice of first job.

Shared management learning

The links between graduate development and management development seem to be strengthening, even in organisations with rather devolved approaches to graduate recruitment. Three trends seem to be facilitating this.

● It seems widely acknowledged that graduates will have to develop many of the skills on which management development is concentrated, especially the interpersonal skills needed to lead others.

- More modular approaches to delivering management training make it easier for some management training modules to be offered to graduates early in career.

- Management development is often corporately designed, so even in very devolved graduate approaches, the management training modules can be provided from the centre. It adds onto and compliments, rather than threatens, locally-provided job-related training.

Encouraging self-development

Graduates entrants are often being offered more structured support for skill and career development than other groups of staff. This can be justified in terms of accelerating and broadening their learning in the first few years.

However, this approach to development sits uneasily with the self-development ethos of most major employers, even for their managerial workforces.

Employers are therefore seeking to find the right balance between giving graduates structured inputs, and helping them get used to taking responsibility for their own development.

Some of the mechanisms being used for this include:

- more individually-tailored training, demanding that the graduate highlights and acts on their own learning needs

- involving graduate entrants with the design of learning events they will attend

- encouragement for graduates to build their own support networks, through collective graduate events, and encouragement to get to know managers throughout the business

- more active involvement in choosing suitable work placements

- the use of mentors and 'buddies' to get graduates in the habit of seeking informal advice from other people.

4.5 Centralisation versus devolution

The tension between centralised and devolved approaches to graduate recruitment and development is not new. However, we might argue that it has become stronger.

Over the last ten years, people management has become increasingly devolved, both out to units from the centre, and out to line managers from HR. In some organisations, functions such as finance or engineering have become a stronger focus for skill and career development than the business unit. However the 'war for talent', and the use of Internet recruitment ,are powerful forces to re-centralise. This is partly to strengthen the corporate brand in the graduate market, and partly to obtain lower cost and faster speed in processing applications. Where various HR processes are being contracted out or centralised in a shared services function, graduate recruitment seems a likely candidate.

In some organisations, management development has been strengthened through centralisation, although a centralised design is often coupled with devolved delivery for all but the most senior managers. It is quite common for graduate development to be managed by the same central unit responsible for management development.

Centralised approach

Centralised recruitment and development approaches offer:

- stronger brand image in the market, and a stronger career offer to entrants, especially a much wider range of career options during and after the scheme

- more natural links with corporate high-potential identification and development right across the organisation

- a potentially stronger link to overall future business needs, although we have not seen much of this in practice

- advantages for functions that are spread across the business, where numbers in any one division may be small, *eg* finance

- stronger links with management development, which usually has a centralised architecture

- more possibility of a coherent approach right through the IES Graduate Value Chain

- possible cost-benefit in recruitment, and the ability to direct applicants to where they are needed.

Centralised approaches find it harder to offer:

- graduates to meet very specific, especially technical, business needs, and those needing strong links with specialised university departments
- strong buy-in and involvement of local line managers and senior people in business divisions.

Devolved approach

Devolved recruitment and development can offer:

- recruitment and development highly tailored to varied needs in different business divisions
- stronger links with universities in specific disciplines
- earlier real jobs
- clear short-term justification for entrants
- stronger involvement of local managers.

Devolved approaches find it harder to offer:

- a strong brand in the graduate market
- high-quality development of generic skills
- the ability to develop and deploy graduates across the business (local managers tend to hang onto their own)
- links with longer-term and corporate business needs.

A federal approach — some central, some local

The trend seems to be towards a combined approach, where some aspects are managed centrally, and others locally.

Interestingly, we found organisations with highly-centralised recruitment and highly-devolved development, but also others with local recruitment, but some measure of shared development.

Federal arrangements can offer:

- attraction to recruits, by playing up the corporate brand, while offering quite diverse career paths and early real jobs

- recruitment to different skill and quality needs, although this cuts across economies of scale in recruitment and selection
- some shared development, and links with management development in particular.

Federal arrangements can lead to:

- allocation of graduates according to the relative popularity of different business areas, not necessarily their real skill needs
- a gap between the corporate promise and the federally-delivered reality
- limited career development where, once recruited, graduates are managed purely on a local basis
- turf wars over who 'owns' the graduates.

Organisations that need to retain a strong brand in the market seem to be operating some kind of federal model. To work well, there needs to be clear network in the HR or development function linking the centre and the relevant business units or functions. This network needs to address which aspects of career development and training will be co-ordinated, and which purely local. It is also helpful for graduate development to have some senior-level line champions in the business, perhaps in a small cross-business committee — effectively the customers for the graduate entry and development approach.

4.6 Summary

This chapter has explored some of the key issues of policy and practice for employers in graduate recruitment and development. It has highlighted:

- the need to match approaches to graduate recruitment and development with varied business needs for different types of graduates recruits. The rather weak planning processes underpinning decisions on graduate recruitment can make this more difficult.
- aligning entry approaches to the increasingly diverse supply of graduates. There are various approaches being used, but there are strong market pressures to present a strong 'brand' to the market.

- the increased importance of e-recruitment, and the need for research on how it can be used more effectively, especially in self-selection and pre-screening

- the development of an umbrella of schemes that can truly offer varied careers to graduates

- finding the best way of attracting and developing high-potential graduates

- avoiding overselling on the graduate development promise

- getting the balance right between the centre and the line in devolved organisational structures.

5. Overview and Looking Ahead

We finish with a brief overview of the recent trends, and our suggestions of issues that we feel are likely to have more importance in the future.

5.1 Summary of recent trends

Since our earlier study on graduate entry and early careers, in 1990, a number of significant changes have taken place in the graduate labour market and in the way businesses use and develop graduate recruits. There have also been some things which have remained fairly constant.

- A major change in the labour market has been the growth in the graduate population, and also its broader nature. As shown in section 2.1, the main growth in the HE sector took place in the early 1990s, and since then it has slowed down considerably. A key government aim has been to encourage wider participation in HE, from non-traditional groups, in particular more from lower social class backgrounds. The graduate output has become more variable in quality than in the past, and this trend is likely to continue.

- Employer demand for graduates has also continued to grow, but overall has been subject to less annual fluctuations than in the past. In particular, there has been growth in organisations which would not have pitched specifically at the graduate market in the early 1990s, and nowadays, much less domination of the graduate market by relatively few large employers. Recruiters, particularly the larger ones, have increasingly diverse business needs for graduates.

- The recruitment process has not changed much in most respects. In particular, there has been little change in interviews and assessment centres. The big change is at the 'front end' — in the use of the Internet for advertising vacancies, application forms, and to some extent for pre-screening. Also, some organisations have outsourced more, in particular 'candidate handling', mainly because of reduced internal HR resources, but also due to advances in IT.

- There is an increased danger of overselling the job and development offer in order to recruit good graduates, partly because of competition and the slower growth at the 'top end ' of the output, and also because of greater use of IT at the 'front-end'. There are also challenges generally for career management in today's more complex and volatile organisations.

- Planning graduate demand better (identified as a gap in the 1990 IES research) has not developed much, and if anything, we see weaker planning processes for graduate recruitment today. Even where fairly centralised recruitment takes place, the centre merely acts as an 'agency' to recruit against bids made by business streams or functions. Given that longer-term leadership potential is still often a reason for recruiting graduates (and significant resources are put in to seeking out talent), HR planning is an important gap.

- There has been a small shift in the pattern of graduate entry. In our earlier study we saw high-potential schemes, functional entry, professional schemes and direct job recruitment. 'Schemes' are still in evidence, partly because they are so attractive to graduates themselves, and also because they are an effective way for large employers to deal with numbers. Corporate high-potential schemes are still very evident (though with smaller numbers), but the main new trend is a growth in corporate 'umbrella' schemes, where a range of jobs for graduates, careers, and training programmes, exist in a more federal organisational structure.

- The continued, and perhaps increased, importance of a graduate recruitment 'brand' and its promotion is apparent. It is seen as giving competitive advantage, and needed for effective targeting and building relationships with particular universities. Effective targeting is now more established, but this is not exclusively on older, more prestigious universities (though some organisations still focus much of their attention on Oxbridge and a few others with high academic reputations). It also includes those with subject strengths (especially relevant degrees and research), and particular student populations (eg including a few in target list with concentrations of minority ethnic students, to meet a diversity agenda; or recruiting more locally).

- For those with well-known and successful 'brands', who can be inundated with applications from the larger graduate output, effective pre-screening has become a more vital ingredient of a successful graduate strategy. New ways are being sought to improve pre-screening and self-selection (*eg* online, see above), but many are still using traditional academic attainment filters ('A' level scores, 2.1 class of degree).

- The growing global dimension of businesses is seen in the greater emphasis in some, of growing their own 'international leadership'. Truly international graduate recruitment, however, is still on a relatively small scale. Meeting the need for international managers is being handled in different ways through graduate entry schemes.

- There is more variety of development on offer to graduates today, reflecting the growing popularity of shorter, modular courses, and coaching and mentoring. The stronger self-development ethos within companies means graduates are expected to take more control of their own development, especially through inputting to the design of learning programmes and building their own support networks.

- There are still significant tensions within organisations about who 'owns' graduates once they are in and, except in the case of high-potential schemes, which are still more centrally run, we found little evidence of systematically deploying graduates to best effect.

- The increased complexity, and also volatility associated with careers, in many organisations, has made it more difficult to meet new graduates' expectations about career progress.

5.2 Issues for the future

Many of these trends will continue, but looking ahead to the next two to three years, but the main issues on the horizon for employers to be considering now, are:

5.2.1 A changing interface between HE and employment

Current government policy indicates limited expansion of HE in the future, and mostly at the new Foundation-degree level and more work-related HE. Some of the likely developments should help to produce graduates with skills of more immediate relevance to the workplace (*eg* more varied vocational routes into and through higher education, and also the HE curriculum development work on employability, such as SkillsPlus). Students are also likely to have had more previous employment experience, and be more 'work ready'.

On the other hand, this study reinforces the primary interest employers have in the intellectual capacity of their graduate recruits. We can expect to see concerns about quality persist, especially if the sector's output becomes more tiered than it is now, with the emergence of new Foundation-degree graduates, little or no growth in the traditional three-year honours degree output, and a more segmented HE sector (more distinctiveness between the cash-rich internationally-focused, more research-led universities, and the cash-poor, more regionally-focused, mainly teaching universities and colleges). So far, employers have sounded a cautious note about Foundation degrees, as there is some confusion about their intended role and purpose, and the business case for recruiting from this route is still unclear to many employers.

All in all, challenges for employers in trying to locate sufficient numbers and quality of the kind of recruits they want to meet their needs, seem likely to remain.

5.2.2 Tight market for some disciplines

There is no good evidence that problems with maths and physics, and therefore with engineering and some other sciences, are not going to disappear in the short term. Employers can therefore expect continuing shortages in such subjects, and need to consider how to reduce their effects, say by offering conversion training, perhaps in conjunction with universities, or by developing their own corporate degrees or other qualifications. Strong links with university departments are advantageous in such tight markets.

5.2.3 Increasing international mobility

The international labour market, as driven by demand from employers for graduate for international appointments (or for professional or management roles requiring experience of other countries), is still slow to develop, and small in scale. But young people are travelling much more, studying more outside their home countries, and we should expect that more will work in other countries in early adulthood. Furthermore, the enlargement of the European Community will substantially widen the talent pool of people who may be attracted to working in the UK, or for UK companies. It is to be expected that our UK graduate labour market will gradually become more international. Advantages will accrue to employers who learn to use this wider talent pool effectively. On the other hand, the UK will also be competing more to retain our own young people in this country, and with some well-known negatives (*eg* climate, housing costs), the offer of really good quality jobs and early career development will be key factors.

5.2.4 The need to evaluate online selection

We have already seen in this study the impact of Internet recruitment, with some organisations attracting far more applicants than they really want, and others finding it difficult to create a strong enough brand to attract candidates. These trends will continue. There is an urgent need for research on the effectiveness of e-recruitment in attracting the right candidates, and in particular of pre-screening electronically.

5.2.5 Delivering imaginative development

If anything, the development offer has become more important in graduate entry, not just in schemes but also for those going directly into jobs. Students will have seen more varied forms of learning in school and HE, and become more familiar with these, and with the idea of 'learning to learn'. They are also more used to using IT to access information, and to get feedback in assessment. They are likely to enter employment with higher expectations, not just of the quantity of development, but more of its quality and ability to be tailored to their individual needs. It is likely that more will expect mentors and project working (dominant in many university courses), and support for obtaining further qualifications. They will be more demanding of support for career development, and will resist the attempts sometimes made in organisations to limit their career movement across business streams, functions or locations.

References

AGR (2002), *Graduate Salaries and Vacancies (Half yearly Review, June 2002)*, AGR/IES

AGR (2003), *Graduate Salaries and Vacancies 2002/03*, AGR

Argyris C (1998), 'Empowerment: The Emperor's New Clothes', *Harvard Business Review*, May-June

Argyris C, Schon D A (1974), *Theory in Practice: Increasing Professional Effectiveness*, Jossey-Bass

Arnold J (1997), *Managing Careers into the 21st Century*, London: Paul Chapman

Bass B M (1985), *Leadership and Performance Beyond Expectations*, London: Free Press

Brewster C, Harris H (eds) (1999), *International HRM: Contemporary issues in Europe*, London: Routledge

Callender C (2003), *Attitudes to Student Debt*, Universities UK and HEFCE

Carter A (2001), *Executive Coaching: Inspiring Performance at Work*, IES Report 379

CEML (2002), *The Contribution of the UK Business Schools to Developing Managers and Leaders*, London: Council for Excellence in Management and Leadership

CIPD (2001), *Career Tracking: Graduate Workplace Attitudes*, Chartered Institute of Personnel and Development, September, 2001

Clutterbuck D, Megginson D (1999), *Mentoring Executives and Directors*, Oxford: Butterworth-Heinemann

Connor H, Strebler M, Hirsh W (1991), *You and Your Graduates: the First Few Years*, IMS (IES) Report 191

Connor H, Pollard E (1996), *What do Graduates Really do?*, IES Report 308, Institute for Employment Studies

Connor H, Burton R, Pearson R, Pollard E, Regan J (1999), *Making the Right Choice: How Students Choose Universities and Colleges*, Universities UK

Connor H, Dewson S (2001), *Social Class and Higher Education: issues affecting decisions on participation by lower social class groups*, DFEE Research Report RR267, London

Connor H, Tyers C, Tackey N, Davis S (2003), *Minority Ethnic Students in Higher Education: an interim report*, DFES Research Report RR448

CSU (2002), *A Review of the latest graduate employment research (Autumn 2002)*, Careers Services Unit (www.csuprospects.ac.uk)

Dearing Review (1997), Report of the National Committee of Inquiry into Higher Education, HMSO

DfES (2003), *The Future of Higher Education*, White Paper, Department for Education and Skills, London, January 2003

DfES and DTI (2002), *Managers and Leaders: Raising our Game*. Government response to the report of the Council for Excellence in Management and Leadership

Elias P, Purcell K, Simms C (1999), *Moving On — graduate careers three years after graduation*, DFEE/AGCAS/CSU/IER

Goleman D (1996), *Emotional Intelligence*, London: Bloomsbury

GradFacts (2002), *The Guardian*

Harvey L, Moon S, Geall V (1997), *Graduates' Work: Organisational Changes and Students' Attributes*, Association of Graduate Recruiters (AGR)

Hesketh A J (2000), 'Recruiting from an elite? Employers' perceptions of graduate education and training', *Journal of Education and Work*, Vol. 13, No. 3

Hillage J, Pollard E (1998), *Employability: Developing a framework for policy analysis*, DfES Research Report RR85

Hiltrop J M (1998), 'Preparing people for the future', *Strategic Change*, Vol. 7, No. 4, June-July, pp. 213-221

Hirsh W, Carter A (2002), *New Directions in Management Development*, IES Report 387

Honey P, Mumford A (1982), *The Manual of Learning Styles*, TMPL Training

IRS (1998), 'Graduate Recruitment and Sponsorship: The 1998 Survey of Employer Practice', *Employee Development Bulletin*, No. 107, November

Jenner S, Taylor S (2000), *Recruiting, Developing and Retaining Graduate Talent*, HR-expert, Pearson Education

Kerrin M, Kettley P (2003), *e-Recruitment: Is it Delivering?*, IES Report 402

King Z (2003), 'New or traditional careers? A study of UK graduates' preferences', *Human Resource Management Journal*, Vol. 13, No. 1, 2003

Knight P, Yorke M (2001), *Employability Through the Curriculum*, Skills Plus Project, Open University, March 2001

National Inquiry Committee into Higher Education (1997), *Higher Education in the Learning Society*, (The Dearing Report), London: NICHE/HMSO

Park Human Resources/GEE (2002), *Graduates in the Eyes of Employers* (GEE), Leeds

Pearson R, Perryman S (2002), *IES Annual Review 2002, Part 1: Higher Education: the new Status Quo; Part 2: Graduates' Early Careers*, IES Report 393

Perryman (2003), *IES Annual Review 2003: Business as Usual? Trends in student and graduate numbers*, IES Report 399

Perryman S, Pollard E, Hillage J, Barber L (2003), *Choices and Transitions: a study of the graduate labour market in the South West*, HERDA-SW

Purcell K, Hogarth T, Pitcher J, Jacobs C (1999), *Graduate Opportunities, Social Class and Age*, IER, April

Purcell K, Pitcher J, Simm C (1999), *Working Out? Early career outcomes in the new graduate labour market*, Manchester, CSU

Purcell K, Morley M, Rowley, G (2002), *Recruiting a Wider Spectrum of Graduates*, CIHE

Rolfe H (2001), *The Effects of Tuition Fees on Students' Demands and Expectations: evidence form case studies of four universities*, Discussion Paper 190, NIESR, December

Saratoga (1998), AGR Benchmarking Survey, 1997-98, *Lancaster: Saratoga Europe*

Sturges J, Guest, D (1999), Should I Stay or Should I go? Issues Relating to the Retention of Graduate Recruits, *The Association of Graduate Recruiters*

Tyers C, Perryman S, Barber L (2003), *Measuring Up: Benchmarking Graduate Retention*, IES Report 401

Universum (1999), *Universum Graduate Survey*, Universum Communications, Sweden

Viney C, Adamson S, Doherty N (1997), 'Paradoxes of Fast Track Career Management', *Personnel Review*, 26(3), pp. 174-186

Waterman R, Waterman J, Collard B (1994), 'Towards a Career Resilient Workforce', *Harvard Business Review*, July-August, pp. 87-95

Winter J, Jackson C (1999), *Riding the Wave*, Oxford, Career Innovation Research Group

Winterton J, Parker M, Dodd M, McCracken M, Henderson I (2000), *Future Skills Needs of Managers*, DfES Research Report RR 182

Wistreich A (2002), *The European Student Survey 2002*, Cambridge, Hobsons